Building Strong Writers in Middle School

Classroom-Ready Activities That Inspire Creativity and Support Core Standards

Deb Delisle and Jim Delisle

free spirit
PUBLISHING®

Library of Congress Cataloging-in-Publication Data
Delisle, Deb, 1953–
Building strong writers in middle school : classroom-ready activities that inspire creativity and support core standards / Deb Delisle and Jim Delisle.
 p. cm.
Includes index.
ISBN 978-1-57542-370-8
 1. English language—Composition and exercises—Study and teaching (Middle school) 2. Curriculum planning. I. Delisle, James R., 1953– II. Title.
 LB1623.D38 2010
 808'.0420712—dc22
 2011003539

eBook ISBN: 978-1-57542-703-4

Free Spirit Publishing does not have control over, or assume responsibility for, author or third-party websites and their content. At the time of this book's publication, all facts and figures cited within are the most current available. All telephone numbers, addresses, and website URLs are accurate and active; all publications, organizations, websites, and other resources exist as described in this book; and all have been verified as of February 2011. If you find an error or believe that a resource listed here is not as described, please contact Free Spirit Publishing. Parents, teachers, and other adults: We strongly urge you to monitor children's use of the Internet.

Photo Credits: cover © JGI/JamieGrill/Blend, blendimages.com • keyboard key (used throughout) © istockphoto.com/jbrizendine • pencil (ued throughout) © Karam Miri | Dreamstime.com • page 52, Siddhartha Guatama illustration © Henry.Lee (Own work) [Public domain], via commons.wikimedia.org from Wikimedia Commons • page 132, photo collage; © istockphoto.com/ZoneCreative, istockphoto.com/Nisangha, istockphoto.com/Dizeloid, istockphoto.com/gsmcity, istockphoto.com/Tatik22

Edited by Eric Braun
Cover and interior design by Tasha Kenyon

10 9 8 7 6 5 4 3 2 1
Printed in the United States of America

Free Spirit Publishing Inc.
217 Fifth Avenue North, Suite 200
Minneapolis, MN 55401-1299
(612) 338-2068
help4kids@freespirit.com
www.freespirit.com

As a member of the Green Press Initiative, Free Spirit Publishing is committed to the three Rs: Reduce, Reuse, Recycle. Whenever possible, we print our books on recycled paper containing a minimum of 30% post-consumer waste. At Free Spirit it's our goal to nurture not only children, but nature too!

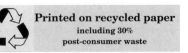

Printed on recycled paper
including 30%
post-consumer waste

Dedication

This book is dedicated to Steve Hegner, colleague, mentor, and friend. Your inspiration, guidance, and support helped me become a better educator and human. Our students' voices are embedded with these lessons.

—DD

This book is dedicated to Dave Ciborek, a colleague, a friend, a mentor, and a fellow traveler on this road of words. Dave, you are the best teacher I have ever known.

—JD

Acknowledgments

We thank the thousands of students whose paths have crossed ours. Due to their talents, intensities, and commitment to wonder, we learned how to turn students' voices into lessons of life.

Too, we thank Eric Braun for his tireless contributions to making our book the best it could be. Editors often have thankless jobs, so from the both of us, sincere gratitude for your care and commitment to our book and to our voice.

Contents

List of Reproducible Pages

Introduction
Inviting Students to Be Strong Writers

As students transition from their early years of schooling to young adolescence, a rush of new emotions and thoughts leads them into a period of exploration and uncertainty. They yearn to fit in and find meaning in their lives, they question their places in the world—and they can easily become self-absorbed.

By no means is this transitional process bad. Self-examination is an important part of growing up, and it is at the heart of this book. The activities in *Building Strong Writers in Middle School* invite students to look inward before expressing their feelings or insights externally. Time and again, we have witnessed students respond in absolutely remarkable ways to assignments that feel personal to them. Not only have our students impressed us with their work, they often have astounded themselves with their creations. We wrote this book because we want your students to share these successes, too.

The Inviting Ways of Invitational Education

Tapping into your students' desire to express themselves is one part of building strong writers in middle school. When done as part of a larger effort to invite students to realize their potential, we see it is the *students* who do the building, not us. This is called invitational education.

William Purkey described his theory of invitational teaching and learning in his 1978 book *Inviting School Success: A Self-Concept Approach to Teaching and Learning,* which he coauthored with John Novak. Still relevant today, invitational education is, in essence, a learning culture in which people are "cordially, creatively, and consistently summoned to realize their potential."

Teachers can do this by setting classroom rules and procedures that are respectful in nature—for instance, more "here's what will happen if you behave" instead of "here's your punishment if you misbehave" statements. Or, in designing curriculum, teachers can first ask themselves, "What options will I provide for my students who either excel at or struggle with this concept?" and then design specific activities that accommodate these students' varied rates of learning. Thus, by personalizing learning, we tell students we value their differences and are willing to support them as they discover their talents and interests.

Invitational education is anchored in five principles:
- respect (believing your students are valuable and capable)
- trust (believing education is a cooperative and collaborative process)
- care (believing the process is as important as the product)
- optimism (believing that students will respond and can succeed)
- intentionality (deliberately looking for ways to invite students to realize their potential)

In essence, an "Intentional Inviter" is someone who designs a culture of learning that is respectful and learning activities that are individually challenging and meaningful for students. The idea of invitational teaching and learning is simple, really, and we made it the basis of our classroom actions—and of the activities in this book.

Using This Book

Building Strong Writers in Middle School is divided into four sections, each containing activities that invite your students to create writing samples that vary in content, style, and length. The first section, "Writing to Get to Know Each Other," contains short activities that will help students introduce themselves to their classmates and vice versa. Most will not require much research beyond students exploring their own ideas or those of family members. Many of this section's activities are best done near the beginning of the school year, or at any other time when you want your students to understand one another more deeply.

The second section, "Writing to Understand Ourselves," requires more intensive and extensive writing from students: "Intensive" in the sense that students will need to explore their personal beliefs and ideas in completing their assignments, and "extensive" meaning more than one classroom session (or work completed as homework) will be required to finish the activities. These assignments work best once your students are already acquainted with one another, since a level of mutual trust among students will likely allow them to be more candid and open in their responses.

"Writing to Make a Difference," the book's third section, includes activities in which students embrace the larger world by acknowledging people who have impacted their lives and/or sharing their finished products with others who may be positively affected by the projects. These activities can be completed whenever, although some teachers prefer to use them in close proximity to holidays, when being thankful or reflective is often a part of holiday festivities.

The book's fourth section, "Writing to Create Art," includes activities that use a visual motif as well as a written one in the final student product. As with many of the other activities in this book, students are asked to be introspective and write about issues or topics of personal importance to them. This section's activities involve a form of literary expression (such as fiction, poetry, and song lyrics), so you may want to undertake these activities at any time during the school year when literature is being studied or simply when you want your students to take a break from their more formal essays, book reports, or extended responses.

Each activity begins with a brief introduction that provides summary and background for the activity. This serves as a way to get a quick handle on the theme and content of the activity. This is followed by the recommended product students will produce, the materials needed to conduct the activity, the time required, and the Common Core State Standards the activity meets (see the corresponding standards chart on page 5). Of course, you may always alter the product based on your students' interests and creativity and your desire to differentiate instruction.

Each activity has three basic steps:

- **The Hook.** This is an engaging way to get students interested in the activity you are about to introduce.

- **Introduce the Activity.** In this step, you'll explain the requirements of the activity and answer any questions students have.

- **Invite Students to Complete Their Own Responses.** This section may contain step-by-step instructions on administering the activity, including, when appropriate, walking you through the stages of drafting, revising, and "publishing," or sharing final products with an audience (often just the class).

Each activity ends with three types of extensions:

- **Classroom Extensions.** Get greater value out of the activity by modifying or expanding it with your students.

- **School Extensions.** Get your whole grade, team, or school involved by opening up the activity in ways that include other students and staff.

- **Family Extensions.** Invite families to be part of the project, and learn from each other by asking them to participate in the activities.

Every activity includes sample assignments written by our students that you may use as models to introduce the activity to your students. We suggest projecting these from your computer onto a screen or interactive white board, using a document camera to project a printout, or creating a transparency. The student samples we have included reflect high-quality writing. While not every one of our students produced work of this caliber (which may also be the case in your classroom), we believe these exemplars may spur your students to create written products that show sophisticated and deep thinking. In the materials list, such items are referred to as "display copies."

A Word About Holistic Evaluation

We are cognizant of the many ways in which students might be assessed in terms of their growth as writers as well as meeting the standards for their particular grade levels. We recognize that assessment is an area of much debate and continued research, so we leave it to you, the teacher, to establish how your students should be evaluated in conjunction with your school's curriculum and expectations. Our recommendation, however, is holistic evaluation.

Holistic evaluation asks the teacher and student to be partners in making sure that the work submitted is meaningful to the person who wrote it and understandable to those who read it, while simultaneously meeting the goals and intended outcomes of the activity. If a piece of work is not as strong or clear as it might be, a holistic evaluator would return it to the student with specific questions and comments designed to strengthen the content, such as, "You went from not making the team in fifth grade to being team captain in seventh grade. What happened that made the difference?" If the grammar, syntax, or sentence structure is confusing, explain to the student that off-the-mark mechanics take away from the story's power and interfere with its flow. Then, ask the student to try to find some errors independently, or ask if she or he needs help from you or a classmate to do so.

If a student submission has some especially strong aspects to it, it is important to comment on them, as students need to understand their strengths and be prepared to replicate them in future writings. When students merely get an "A" or a "Great job," they cannot differentiate between strengths and weaknesses in their writing. It's also beneficial for students to read one another's work in pairs or small groups, providing compliments and suggestions for improvement. Guiding discussion topics such as the following can greatly assist students in their peer discussions:

- This is what I really like about this piece of writing.

- This is one part that confused me.

- I think you can make your writing stronger by . . .

As teachers, of course we need to know what grade to put in the grade book, and students need to know on the front end of any activity how they will be assessed. We suggest that effort and the actual process of completing the assignment be a strong component of whatever assessment is employed. So, if a letter grade is required in your situation, be sure to let students know what constitutes an A, a B, and so forth.

Some of the best assessments are those designed by students and teachers collaboratively. By sharing the intended outcomes of the activity, you can engage students in the development of rubrics and even scoring guides. You may also ask students some important questions following the activity, such as: What did you learn about yourself as a writer by completing this activity? Such insights can help you develop future activities that meet student needs.

You also benefit your students greatly when you encourage them to write for a purpose other than receiving a grade or fulfilling a requirement, such as publication in magazines and on websites, recognition in district-wide collections of exemplary writing, or the creation of a school-wide literary journal. This helps students recognize the power of sharing their ideas and the many purposes writing can serve.

If we ever get to the point where the only activities we do in schools are those that are so concrete they can be reduced to a single letter or number grade, we have lost sight of the fact that some of school's—and life's—best learning moments cannot be distilled into a simplistic score. Some activities are inherently worthwhile and demand a narrative response from a teacher. Even a student who earns a "Super job!" comment needs to understand what specifically she or he did well, so it can be repeated in future writing.

These Activities Align with the Common Core State Standards

Education in the United States has changed significantly in the past decade, stemming from increased demands for accountability, higher standards, and supportive learning environments filled with rigorous and relevant learning activities. In 2009 and 2010, a national initiative led by states emerged to identify what it is students should know and be able to do in English/language arts and mathematics. The resulting work yielded a set of comprehensive standards in English/language arts (ELA) and mathematics that do not tell teachers how to teach but rather that identify knowledge and skills essential in each of the two content areas. These Common Core State Standards rely on educators to determine how to best translate these standards into rigorous learning experiences that consider the needs of their students, the expectations of the communities in which they work, and the available resources to support students in their learning.

As the chart on page 5 shows, the activities in this book align with the Common Core State Standards for ELA. Using these activities in your curriculum will assist your students in strengthening their writing and communication skills. The activities will easily align with your district's adopted course of study, model curriculum, or your state's requirements. The activities are designed to extend students' thinking and deepen their skills in the essential process of communicating effectively.

The Common Core State Standards are based upon research that identifies skills essential to the writing process. Although the chart on page 5 identifies specific Common Core State Standards that align with each activity, the activities will most likely align with your state's standards as well, if your state has not adopted the Common Core State Standards.

Building an Appreciation for Writing

Something within the human condition implores us to communicate. We write, we talk, we sing, we read, we listen, we dance, we cheer, we karaoke (often badly), and we use every

Activities Aligned with Common Core State Standards

	Common Core State Standard: **Writing**	Activity #
1	Write narratives to develop real or imagined experiences or events using effective techniques, relevant descriptive details, and well-structured event sequences.	9, 11, 12, 16, 17
2	Produce clear and coherent writing in which the development, organization, and style are appropriate to task, purpose, and audience.	1–9, 11–24
3	With some guidance and support from peers and adults, develop and strengthen writing as needed by planning, revising, editing, rewriting, or trying a new approach.	1–9, 11–24
4	Use technology, including the Internet, to produce and publish writing as well as to interact and collaborate with others; demonstrate sufficient command of keyboarding skills to type a minimum of three pages in one sitting.	3–9, 11–24
5	Draw evidence from literary or informational texts to support analysis, reflection, and research.	9
6	Write routinely over extended time frames (time for research, reflection, and revision) and shorter time frames (a single sitting or a day or two) for a range of discipline-specific tasks, purposes, and audiences.	3–9, 11–24
	Common Core State Standard: **Reading**	Activity #
7	Determine a theme or central idea of a text and how it is conveyed through particular details; provide a summary of the text distinct from personal opinions or judgments.	11, 12, 17, 20–24
8	Determine the meaning of words or phrases as they are used in a text, including figurative and connotative meanings; analyzing the impact of specific word choice on meaning or tone.	11, 12, 20–24
9	Analyze how a particular sentence, chapter, scene, or stanza fits into the overall structure of a text and contributes to the development of the theme, plot, or setting.	23, 24
10	Explain how an author develops the point of view of the narrator or speaker in a text.	9
11	Compare and contrast the experience of reading a story, drama, or poem to listening to or viewing an audio, video, or live version of the text, including contrasting what they "see" and "hear" when reading the text to what they perceive when they listen or watch.	22
	Common Core State Standard: **Speaking and Listening**	Activity #
12	Engage effectively in a range of collaborative discussions (one-on-one, in groups, and teacher-led) with diverse partners on topics, texts, and issues, applicable to specific grade level, building on others' ideas and expressing their own clearly.	All
13	Adapt speech to a variety of contexts and tasks, demonstrating command of formal English when indicated or appropriate.	4, 12
	Common Core State Standard: **Language**	Activity #
14	Demonstrate command of the conventions of standard English grammar and usage when writing or speaking.	All
15	Demonstrate command of the conventions of standard English capitalization, punctuation, and spelling when writing.	All
16	Use knowledge of language and its conventions when writing, speaking, reading, or listening.	All
17	Determine or clarify the meaning of unknown and multiple-meaning words and phrases based on grade-level requirements, choosing flexibly from a range of strategies.	3, 8, 16, 18–24
18	Demonstrate understanding of figurative language, word relationships, and nuances in word meanings.	2, 3, 7, 8, 12, 15, 16, 18–24
19	Acquire and use accurately grade-appropriate general academic and domain-specific words and phrases; gather vocabulary knowledge when considering a word or phrase important to comprehension or expression.	1–4, 7, 8, 11, 12, 16–24

manner of verbal or physical expressions we can to get others to receive the stories we each contain. Voices memorialized on paper or sent into cyberspace seem to have a permanence not possible with the spoken word. Each essay, song lyric, reflection, or poem that we produce can last the eternity that we are not privileged to share. Decades—even centuries—from today, a new reader might pick up this or any other book and learn something about the long-ago world. Such is the power of the written word. That is why the art of writing is one of the most essential journeys we can share with our students and guide them to master.

A love for writing and a true understanding of the longevity of the written word takes time. To help develop this love and understanding, the activities in this book contain the following elements:

- **Personal expression.** The voices of our students are of utmost importance. Especially in early adolescence, there is both a need and a desire to talk about one's self and one's views of the world. Providing our students with a legitimate forum to express these ideas not only validates their opinions and insights, it also validates them as human beings. One of the greatest gifts we can give our students is to treat their words and their work with respect and dignity.

- **Open-endedness.** When we assign classroom activities, many students want to know the "right" way of completing them. The age-old request, "Just tell me what you're looking for," is the student's plea to grasp not only the purpose of our assignments, but also the preferred format, length, and style. We appreciate these students' desire to be both accurate and articulate, yet, simultaneously, we want them to express themselves in unique ways.

- **Integration.** Just as every person has a mind and a heart, the activities here provide opportunities for students to write from cognitive knowledge and emotional sensation. Not every student is equally skilled or enthusiastic when it comes to putting pen to paper or fingers to keyboard, and some students write freely about their inner selves while others are more reticent. This is why these activities allow for students to complete them with various levels of depth and knowledge.

- **Fun.** Not "enjoyment" or "pleasure" . . . *fun!* In this era of data-driven everything in our schools, the simple joy of playing around with ideas and words is increasingly left on the instructional sidelines. Lessons that are not measurable by some standardized something-or-other are given short-shrift by those overly concerned with accountability. However, we know this: Having fun while writing and sharing with others can result in some very special—and valuable—and educational—outcomes.

We always find great joy in students' work. So, please feel free to share some of your students' writing, or even your own experiences, by writing or emailing us in care of the address below. We'd love to hear from you.

Happy writing!
—Deb and Jim Delisle

Free Spirit Publishing
217 Fifth Avenue North, Suite 200
Minneapolis, MN 55401-1299
help4kids@freespirit.com

Writing to Get to Know Each Other

The goal of these activities is to help you and your students, with whom you share almost 200 days each year, get to know each other better. Though you can do these activities during the opening week of school (when most "getting to know you" activities are typically completed), they are all appropriate for any other time of the year, too. Each activity allows students to share personal parts of themselves: their interests, dreams, fears, regrets, and joys. You and your students will find yourselves laughing, pondering, and learning more about each other.

Each of the following activities will take 30 minutes or less to explain, complete, and discuss, making them perfect for opening or closing the school week. Also, doing these activities after an especially arduous day (perhaps a morning filled with standardized testing) can relax the tenor of the classroom, making for great transitional activities for students in need of a change of pace or tone.

In today's standards-based classrooms, every lesson seems designed to correlate with a curriculum goal that relates to content, content, content, and all the activities in this book are correlated to the Common Core State Standards for English/language arts (see page 5). But classroom activities that help students and teachers get to know each other from the inside out also have value. For us, this section's activities have been effective in reaching our students in ways that tests and quizzes never could.

Learning Objectives

- To allow students the opportunity to consider those personal qualities, quirks, and interests that make them unique

- To help students discover the similarities and differences they share with classmates

- To help students appreciate the unique elements and interests of classmates they probably thought they knew well already

1. Getting to Know You—Better

There is no better way to learn interesting things about your students than to ask them questions about their sometimes serious, sometimes funny, sometimes quirky lives. This activity, which is ideal for the first week of school, engenders both rich emotions and genuine guffaws—both of which are necessary in a memorable school year. Best of all, when the activity is complete, you all will have learned information about each other as people, not just as students and teachers.

Product	A completed short-answer questionnaire that students will share orally with the class
Materials	• 1 copy of the "Getting to Know You—Better" questionnaire (page 11) for each student • 1 display copy of the "Getting to Know You—Better" sample student response (page 12) • 1 display copy of the "Getting to Know You—Better" selection of possible answers from Mickey Mouse and Rosa Parks (page 13) • *Optional:* A copy of the last page from an issue of *Vanity Fair* magazine or an excerpt from the "questioning segment" on the television show *Inside the Actors Studio* and a DVD player
Time	30–45 minutes
Common Core State Standards	Activity meets standards 2, 3, 12, 14, 15, 16, and 19 from the chart on page 5.

Activity Steps

1. The Hook

As straight-faced as possible, look around your classroom and, one by one, ask random students one of the following questions:

- What's your favorite word?
- What's your least favorite word?
- What's your favorite sound?
- What's your least favorite sound?

Be prepared for students to say, "I don't have a favorite word." At this point, walk over to the nonresponsive student and say (as seriously as you can muster), "Of course you do . . . everyone has one. Why, mine is *hypoallergenic*."

Most students will laugh a bit, or look to each other with raised eyebrows wondering where their normal teacher went. This is the perfect atmosphere in which to conduct this activity.

2. Introduce the Activity

Now that you have your students' attention, you can go one of several ways to introduce this activity. If you have a copy of the last page of a *Vanity Fair* magazine (called the "Proust Questionnaire"), you may share it with your students. On this page, famous actors, politicians, entrepreneurs, or musicians answer the types of questions that will be listed on the blank questionnaires that your students will complete. Most of the individuals highlighted on the pages from *Vanity Fair* will not be people your students know, but that is not as big an issue as getting them to listen to some of the insights shared in the responses.

Alternatively, if you have access to a DVD of one of the *Inside the Actors Studio* episodes, go to the final ten-minute segment where host James Lipton asks his famous guests the same type of questions that appear on the Proust Questionnaire. (**Warning:** Watch the video before showing it to your class and be prepared to skip over the question, "What is your favorite curse word?") Watching this brief segment gives your students some powerful examples of interesting responses.

If you have access to neither of the above, you can use the speculative answers provided (page 13) for a fictional character (Mickey Mouse) and a historic one (Rosa Parks) as a springboard for your conversation. You can choose other figures and provide the answers you believe the figures would give or ask your students to speculate how the figures would respond.

If you wish, share the responses given by a seventh grader, Pav, as he relates his answers to his own life (page 12). This real-world example might be helpful for students who worry that their lives are not quite as interesting as the famous person examples you have shown to them.

3. Invite Students to Complete Their Own Responses

Distribute the blank "Getting to Know You—Better" questionnaire (page 11) to your students and go over it with them. Ask if there are any questions. Before students start answering their questionnaires, let them know that they will be sharing some answers with the class. Have a class vote—or else decide ahead of time—which of these two ways they will share:

1. Students know in advance that classmates can feel free to ask for elaboration on a particular response.

2. Students agree that whatever responses they write will be "stand alone," and no one can ask them to explain their response further.

Both modes can be intriguing. If it is agreed that anyone can ask about responses, students may be more guarded in writing something of a personal nature. However, if students know that their responses will not be questioned, they may permit themselves to take a risk in writing something they might not otherwise share. As long as all agree to the form of sharing that will take place once the answers are written, the discussion at this activity's end will be rich and rewarding.

Once these ground rules have been established, have your students begin responding to their questionnaires. Tell them they may answer the questions in any order, and they are not required to answer every single question. (Most will want to answer every item, but giving an "out" allows for students not to reveal anything that might be embarrassing or too personal.)

Ask students not to talk with classmates as they complete this sheet, since responses tend to get less personal and more "cookie cutter" when everyone is sharing what they are writing.

Allow 10 to 15 minutes for students to complete their questionnaires, then ask each student to share one or two answers under the guidelines you've established.

Note: To encourage your students to open up in their responses—and to help build a sense of community—complete the "Getting To Know You—Better" questionnaire when they do, and share your answers under the same ground rules.

Extensions

Classroom Extensions

1. If you have a class list of students before school opens, send them the "Getting to Know You—Better" questionnaire in advance of the first day of school and request that they bring the completed forms with them on the first day, at which time you can use them as an icebreaker.

2. If you do a biography unit sometime during the school year, have students complete the "Getting to Know You—Better" sheet from the vantage point of the person whose life they have studied. Display these in a hallway, on a classroom bulletin board, or on a class website alongside a picture of the biography subject.

School Extension

At a faculty meeting near the beginning of the year, distribute blank copies of the "Getting to Know You—Better" questionnaire, collecting the completed questionnaires at the end of the meeting. Then, at subsequent meetings or weekly email staff bulletins, reveal a particular teacher, administrator, or staff member's responses to several of the items, seeing if other members of the school family can figure out who wrote what. Of course, give everyone the right to opt out of this public revelation.

Family Extension

At Open House night, put together a "composite class portrait" of selected responses to these questions and share them with families (do not select answers that would make the student-author's identity obvious to his or her family). Use this as a springboard to discuss just how diverse your class is in terms of interests, fears, passions, and aspirations. Leave each parent with a blank copy of the "Getting to Know You—Better" questionnaire, inviting them to complete the form at home and share their responses with their children, who, likewise, can share their own responses.

Getting to Know You—Better

1. What is your favorite word?
   _____

2. What is your least favorite word?
   _____

3. What is your favorite sound?
   _____
   _____
   _____
   _____

4. What is your least favorite sound?
   _____
   _____
   _____
   _____

5. What would make you as happy as possible?
   _____
   _____
   _____
   _____

6. What trait or behavior of yours do you most dislike?
   _____
   _____
   _____
   _____

7. What trait or behavior do you most dislike in others?
   _____
   _____
   _____
   _____

8. What is your greatest regret?
   _____
   _____
   _____
   _____

9. What is your most cherished possession?
   _____
   _____
   _____
   _____

10. What is your greatest fear?
    _____
    _____
    _____
    _____

11. If you could live anywhere, where would it be?
    _____
    _____

12. What do you value the most in your friends?
    _____
    _____
    _____
    _____

13. Whom do you most admire?
    _____
    _____
    _____

14. What is it that you most dislike?
    _____
    _____
    _____

15. What is your favorite smell?
    _____
    _____

Your name _____

From *Building Strong Writers in Middle School: Classroom-Ready Activities That Inspire Creativity and Support Core Standards* by Deb Delisle and Jim Delisle, copyright © 2011.
Free Spirit Publishing Inc., Minneapolis, MN; 800-735-7323; www.freespirit.com. This page may be reproduced for use within an individual school or district.
For all other uses, contact www.freespirit.com/company/permissions.cfm.

Getting to Know You—Better

Sample Student Response, *Pav, 7th grade*

3. What is your favorite word?

   Blubber

4. What is your least favorite word?

   "often" with the 't' sounded out

5. What is your favorite sound?

   That satisfying click that you get sometimes when two things fit perfectly together

6. What is your least favorite sound?

   The slurping of soup

7. What would make you as happy as possible?

   Feeling that whatever happens doesn't matter because I have everything okay in my life

8. What trait or behavior of yours do you most dislike?

   I am shy around other people who I know don't think much of me

9. What trait or behavior do you most dislike in others?

   Continuous talking

10. What is your greatest regret?

   Not going to India when my grandfather died

11. What is your most cherished possession?

   my talent for writing

12. What is your greatest fear?

   Being Kidnapped

13. If you could live anywhere, where would it be?

   India

14. What do you value the most in your friends?

   Trustworthiness and loyalty

15. Whom do you most admire?

   Jackie Robinson and Doctors Without Borders

16. What is it that you most dislike?

   Mayonnaise and clowns

17. What is your favorite smell?

   Garlic

   Your name Pav

Getting to Know You—Better

Possible Answers from Mickey Mouse

4. What is your least favorite sound?

The snap of a mousetrap

7. What trait or behavior do you most dislike in others?

Tail-pulling

9. What is your most cherished possession?

My autographed photo of Walt Disney

14. Whom do you most admire?

The Make-A-Wish Foundation kids I meet

in my job

Possible Answers from Rosa Parks

1. What is your favorite word?

Courage

9. What is your most cherished possession?

The knowledge that my actions gave others
strength to stand up for their beliefs

10. What is your greatest fear?

That oppressed people will stop striving for their
freedom

12. What do you value the most in your friends?

Being "colorblind" in determining a person's
worthiness

From *Building Strong Writers in Middle School: Classroom-Ready Activities That Inspire Creativity and Support Core Standards* by Deb Delisle and Jim Delisle, copyright © 2011.
Free Spirit Publishing Inc., Minneapolis, MN; 800-735-7323; www.freespirit.com. This page may be reproduced for use within an individual school or district.
For all other uses, contact www.freespirit.com/company/permissions.cfm.

2. Who Knew?

Of all the activities we have done to get to know our students better, few have provided as much new and interesting information as this one. You may also know of similar activities under different names—"Liar's Club," for one—but "Who Knew?" is the one we use with our students. And yes, at various times throughout the year, when something new is learned about a classmate or the teacher, it is not unusual to hear a collective chorus of "Who knew?" arise from the classroom's back rows of desks. So, in addition to being informative, this activity is also lots of fun.

Product	Students write five statements about themselves, one of which is false, and try to guess each other's false statements
Materials	• 1 copy of your own list of five "Who Knew?" responses for each student (four true facts and one lie about yourself) • 1 display copy of the "Who Knew?" student samples (page 17) • Access for all students to any age-appropriate resource for interesting facts, such as the iPhone application "Cool Facts" or a copy of *Who Knew? Things You Didn't Know About Things You Know Well* by David Hoffman
Time	30 minutes
Common Core State Standards	Activity meets standards 2, 3, 12, 14, 15, 16, 18, and 19 from the chart on page 5.

Activity Steps

1. The Hook

Before class, research five facts and write them on the board or project them on the wall for your students to see as they enter the room. Make one of the facts false. Feel free to use the following example:

- Hostess produces 500 million Twinkies each year.

- The U.S state with the longest coastline is Florida.

- Perfume was used a lot in 17th-century Europe because bathing was considered unhealthy and people usually bathed only once a year . . . or even less often.

- A human being's largest organ is the skin.

- The White House in Washington, D.C., was originally gray.

Tell your students that one of these five statements is not true, and ask them to guess which it is (in the example, it's the second "fact": Alaska is the U.S. state with the longest coastline). Next, ask students to volunteer any other interesting trivia they know about the world that others in class may not know. As students list off anomalies or little-known facts, toss in an occasional "Who knew?" to set the tone for what is to follow.

2. Introduce the Activity

Next, shift your class discussion to more personal factoids. For example, ask your students:

- From what nations are your parents, grandparents, or great-grandparents?

- How many different languages do you and your relatives speak?

- In how many different states and nations have you lived?

- What kinds of pets do you have in your home?

Inevitably, there may be a few surprises, an indication, perhaps, of the wide diversity you surely have in your class. To take it a step further, and to get students thinking even deeper about their diversity, show the "Who Knew?" student samples page and discuss them. This can be particularly helpful for those students who feel their lives are dull compared to others'. Students will note that some of the items listed by Sara, Clark, and Melissa are quite ordinary, giving your students permission to list some ideas that are not earth-shattering in any way.

Note: Melissa's lie is #4 (her sister lies all the time, according to Melissa); Clark's lie is #5 (he doesn't have a sister); and Sara's lie is #3 (Sara plays four instruments, not two).

Tell your students: "All of you have interesting tidbits about your experiences and goals that might be surprising for others in class to learn. Even I have some intriguing parts of my past that might surprise you." Then, share the "Who Knew?" handout you created about your own life and ask students to guess which of the five statements on your sheet is false. Finally, tell students it is now their turn to surprise each other.

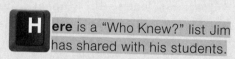

Here is a "Who Knew?" list Jim has shared with his students.

Jim's "Who Knew?" List

1. I had to take over the controls of a small plane when the pilot got sick.

2. I almost drowned when I fell off a boat into the ocean.

3. I like listening to music by Pearl Jam, Etta James, Louis Armstrong, and Green Day.

4. I bought a sports car but didn't know how to use its stick shift and clutch to change gears.

5. I took my first overseas trip by throwing a dart at a world map and traveling where it landed.

(The lie is #1)

3. Invite Students to Complete Their Own Responses

Ask your students to write four truths and one lie on the back of the handout with your list. Allow five minutes to complete this, then proceed one of two ways: have each student read his or her individual statements; or, if the class is large, have students converse in small groups, reporting back only those students who managed to surprise everyone enough that the group said a collective "Who knew?"

Extensions

Classroom Extensions

1. Once the students have read their lists, take a digital photograph of each student and display the students' headshot photographs next to their "Who Knew?" lists. Attach each list to the wall, adjacent to the student's photo, but do not tape the bottom of the list to the wall. Instead, ask students to identify their lies on the backside of the page so others can lift the paper to find out what's true . . . and what isn't. If you have a class website or blog, you can post students' lists and photos there, revealing the lies in a subsequent post. Encourage friends and families to post comments—and guesses—in the comment section.

2. As a team or grade-level activity, assemble your students into the auditorium and have each of their teachers go onstage with their "Who Knew?" lists projected behind them or next to them. Have students indicate which item they believe is a lie for each teacher by applauding when the item is read aloud. When each lie is revealed, have the assembled students shout "Who Knew?" before proceeding to the next teacher. It helps to have an emcee for this—perhaps the school principal—whose "Who Knew?" list can be revealed at the activity's conclusion.

3. Do this activity near the beginning of the year, make copies of each student's list, and put them aside until the school year's end. Then do the activity again without letting students see what they wrote at the beginning of the year. Afterward, have each student compare the early and current lists to see if any more interesting changes or challenges have occurred over a year's time.

4. As new students join your classroom, partner them up with one or two other students and ask these students to explain the "Who Knew?" activity and share their own lists. Then, after the new student has completed his or her list, have the "veteran" students introduce this new classmate to everyone using the "Who Knew?" list.

School Extension

If your school district provides a mentoring program in which new teachers are paired with experienced teachers for a year or more, use the "Who Knew?" activity as an icebreaker during one of the early mentoring meetings. Then, at a time closer to the end of the year, have the new teachers complete another "Who Knew?" list, but this time, each of the items listed must represent something they experienced during that year of teaching. For example, "I called a parent to talk about a behavior problem with their child and realized I'd phoned the wrong parent." Again, one of these statements will be a lie . . . but it may be hard to determine which one it is.

Family Extension

Give the "Who Knew?" activity as "family homework," asking each adult and sibling in the family to complete a "Who Knew?" list. This could also include grandparents and other relatives willing to participate. After the lists are compiled, have each student collect these lists and interview one of the family members whose list was most intriguing to them. The student can then write a brief essay, "The relative I thought I knew."

Sixth Graders' "Who Knew?" Lists

melissa
1. I almost got lost at the Grand Canyon.
2. I hit my head on four metal bars while falling off a jungle gym.
3. I've been to Canada.
4. I have a sister named Stacy who doesn't lie.
5. I know someone who guards the Dalai Lama.

Clark
1. I pulled a fire alarm when I thought it said "free."
2. I cried when my fish got flushed down the toilet.
3. I'm afraid of my grandmother.
4. I can't bend my big toe backward.
5. I named my sister "Rudolph" when she was born.

Name: Sara
1. I'm one of the few girls in my class who has never had a boyfriend.
2. I got my head stuck in a folding chair.
3. I can play two instruments.
4. I'm considering being a teacher for my career.
5. I didn't have hair until I was 3½ years old and then it grew in all white.

3. Visual Enigmas

In some ways, this activity is like others in this section, but the element of artwork involved in "Visual Enigmas" can help attract the attention of reluctant writers and those students who prefer visual art and creativity. To help create a fun and collaborative atmosphere, make your own visual enigma, either beforehand (as an exemplar for students) or at the same time as students are completing theirs.

Product	A visual puzzle of students' first names, supported by five sentences describing themselves
Materials	• 1 sheet of plain white paper per student • 1 sheet of blank, colored paper per student • Rulers, pencils, and thin-lined markers and/or crayons for each student • 1 display copy of the "Optical Illusions" handout (page 21) • 1 display copy of the "Visual Enigmas" handout (page 22) • 1 display copy of the "Visual Enigmas: Sample Student Responses" handout (page 23)
Time	30–40 minutes to introduce, complete, and share this activity
Common Core State Standards	Activity meets standards 2, 3, 4, 6, 12, 14, 15, 16, 17, 18, and 19 from the chart on page 5.

Activity Steps

1. The Hook

Display the optical illusions handout so students see it as they arrive to class. Say nothing to the students about the illusions except that you would like them to look at the illustrations and discuss among themselves what they think they see.

Allow this banter to continue for several minutes, then have a class discussion about what the images are. Here are common interpretations:

a. The capital letter "E"

b. A white question mark or a black-winged bird (like a phoenix)

c. The letters "A," "B," and the beginning of "C"

d. A knight riding a horse or a snowman

e. A dog walking through a field

f. Different from the others, this is a figure that is impossible to build, as it exists only in two dimensions. Prove it by pointing to the top, left round circle, and tracing the illustration to the right. You will end up in hollow space, not solid space.

2. Introduce the Activity

Ask your students what illustrations like these are called. At least a few are bound to say "optical illusions," and, when you get this response, write these two words on the board and ask for definitions or explanations of the phrase.

"Yes," you could say, "the word *optical* has to do with vision—your eyes—while an *illusion* is something you think you see, but it is not real."

Important: Let students know that if they do not see what most people see, or if they don't see a familiar image at all, nothing is wrong with them! This is not a test; rather, it simply shows that the images our eyes give our brains can vary considerably among people. As a way to prove this, ask students who saw things other than <u>the most common</u> <u>responses</u> to state what they saw, pointing out on the image or explaining it orally.

Show them the student samples and briefly discuss each one. Help your students see that one contains the name "Matthew" while the other contains the name "Mandy." Point out that all the letters are connected, and that some of them share common lines (for example, Mandy's "D" is also part of her letter "A.") Finally, point out that each of the visual enigmas is supported by five personal statements about the writer. This is the model they will follow. Students may write about their interests, ambitions, or anything else that makes them interesting or unique.

3. Invite Students to Complete Their Own Responses

Students should be able to create their visual enigma and write the five supporting statements in one class period. Here are some guidelines and helpful hints to make each student's final product look its best:

- Have students first draw their names as visual enigmas in pencil on practice paper.

- Make sure that students use the full top half of the paper for their finished enigma, saving the bottom half of their paper for their five statements. Students often make their enigmas way too small.

- When students are ready to transfer their images onto the colored paper, have them first draw their enigma lightly in pencil. Only after double-checking the size and spelling should they trace over their letters using thin-lined markers or crayons.

- Some students will want to do their last names as well as their first names. If you allow that, make sure they separate the two names or the enigmas will be virtually impossible to decipher.

Once your students have completed their enigmas, display them on a bulletin board or wall just outside your classroom, or scan them and display them on a class website or blog. You may want to post these next to digital headshots of each student for added enjoyment.

Next, tell your students that instead of calling these puzzles "optical illusions," you have another, fancier term for them: *visual enigmas.* At this point, display the "Visual Enigmas" handout, revealing only one word at a time for discussion and interpretation. Each word ("enigma," "quandary," "conundrum," and "mystery") is written in a cryptic form, yet all of the letters of each word are included in the visual enigma. Don't expect that most students will know the words *quandary* or *conundrum*, but do let them know that all of the words on this page are essentially synonymous.

Say: "Just as these words look mysterious and hard to figure out, we might say the same thing about you—that without a little help and explanation, *you* could remain a mystery for much of the year." Explain that the students will create their own visual enigmas to encapsulate this mystery, and they will write five statements about themselves to help unravel that mystery.

Extensions

Classroom Extensions

1. Have students use their completed visual enigmas as covers for whatever organizer they use to keep their papers together. Or, if your classroom desk configuration is such that students face one another, tape each enigma to the front of each child's desk.

2. If your students are enrolled in exploratory foreign language instruction, talk with that teacher to see if students can complete these visual enigmas in the new language they are learning. Not only will your students be interested in what their names are in another language, they will also be able to practice writing a few basic sentences in that language.

3. If your students are involved in a buddy program in which they read to or tutor students in a lower grade, use this activity as a way for students to get to know one another a little better. Your students can help explain what optical illusions are to some children who may not have seen them before.

4. As part of a biography unit you might be teaching, have your students complete a visual enigma for the famous person they are studying. Or, if you are reading young adult literature that has particularly rich characters, students can complete a visual enigma for one or more of the characters in their novels.

School Extension

Delegate one hallway bulletin board with a "Getting to know the staff" theme. Every week, display two different visual enigmas of a teacher, administrator, custodian, or other school staff. A headshot photo could be included, or a "Who is this mysterious person?" option could be done instead, where the first and last names of the person are written as a visual enigma, followed by five statements that help identify the individual behind the enigma. This is an interesting way to introduce all staff members to your school's students. (*Hint:* Enlarge the copy of the visual enigma and statements to accommodate the larger size of the bulletin board.)

Family Extension

If your students do some sort of project during the year that requires them to interview their family members, the visual enigma activity is a fine way to display their results. In the middle of a large poster board, complete a visual enigma of the last name(s) of the family members, with long lines connected to the first names of the family members (again, written as enigmas). Then, list three to five items under each family member's name that helps distinguish him or her from the others.

Optical Illusions

A

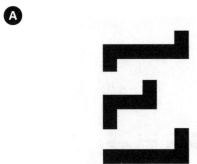

B

C

D

E

F

ENIGMA

QUANDARY

CONUNDRUM

MYSTERY

Visual Enigmas
Sample Student Responses

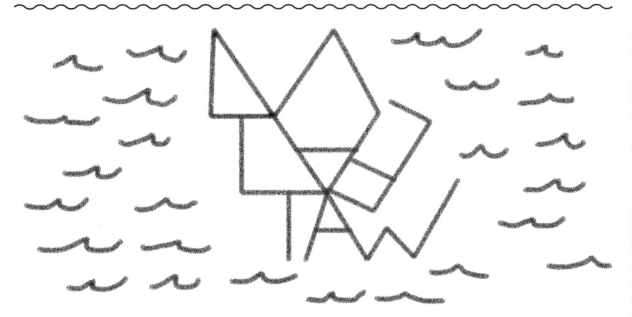

5. My parents are from Romania.

6. I like to fish with my grandfather.

7. I like to read all kinds of books.

8. I like to play pool with my family.

9. I have two sets of grandparents and I love to visit them on weekends.

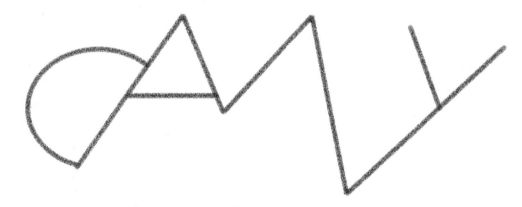

10. I used to be a hippie but I outgrew my tie-dyed T-shirt.

11. I like to try foods that I've never tasted before.

12. My motto is "Cool, calm, and collected."

13. I enjoy listening to Old School and composing rhymes.

14. I love when I get love back.

4. That's Just Like Me!

Like the other activities in this section, this one serves the dual purpose of being fun as well as informative. For some students, the most fun of all may be using a thesaurus to find more complex ways to express things about themselves. Indeed, you could turn this activity into a challenge for all students to find some terms that describe them in ways that sound quite sophisticated!

Product	A "Just Like (student's first name)" poem that contains personal characteristics about the student
Materials	• 1 sheet of blank, lined paper for each student • 1 display copy of the "Just Like Me!" sample student responses (page 27) • Writing and drawing materials for all students • Several print thesauruses or access to an online thesaurus (such as www.merriam-webster.com)
Time	45 minutes
Common Core State Standards	Activity meets standards 2, 3, 4, 6, 12, 13, 14, 15, 16, and 19 from the chart on page 5.

Activity Steps

1. The Hook

Before class, ask one student to be in on the trick you are going to play as you begin this activity.

As students enter the room, tell them to sit at their desks and stay absolutely quiet. Pause intentionally, increasing their interest and curiosity. Mention that you are going to tell them some things about yourself so that they might get to know you a little better. Begin reading (or pretend to read) a selection that sounds something like this (the asterisks are explained below):

"When I was young, I couldn't wait for Friday afternoons to come (★). It wasn't that I didn't like school, it was just that weekends gave me time to do all the things that I never had time for during the week (★). I'd play baseball (★), eat pizza at sleepovers (★) and, when I was

old enough, I'd drive our family car anywhere to have the chance to get behind the wheel of my dad's rusting Ford (★★)"

This may not be the most exciting story, but your "planted" student will help liven it up by standing and exclaiming "Hey! That's just like me!" and immediately sitting back down at the spot of each single asterisk. No doubt, the other students will see this student as either a little wacky or overexcitable. And the double asterisk? That's where your plant stands up and says, "That's not like me *at all*!" Of course, you have to play your part each time the student rises: giving a dirty look, sounding exasperated, and staring quizzically at the offending interrupter.

2. Introduce the Activity

Now that your students are hooked, let your planted student *off* the hook by telling everyone that he or she was playing along with your act. While your story was just for fun, it's now time to turn the class's attention to things that may really be just like them.

Read the following statements, pausing briefly after each one to give students the opportunity to reply: If the item sounds like an interest they have or is something they like to do, they are to stand up immediately, place their arms over their heads and wiggle their fingers, simultaneously saying, "That's just like me!" If they don't agree with the statement or it is not something that interests them, they simply remain seated until the next item is read. Within five minutes, this part of the activity will be over and your students will also have received some exercise. (A bonus!) Here's the list. You may want to add a few questions of your own invention, too.

1. If I could eat only one food, it would be pizza.

2. I want to own a sports car someday.

3. I wish I were older than I am.

4. I want to fly in space someday.

5. I dream in color.

6. I can name all 50 U.S. states.

7. I've known my best friend for longer than one year.

8. I make up my own rules when I play games.

9. I break my own rules when I play a game.

10. I like mud puddles better than bubble baths.

11. I wish I could go to school all year.

12. I know more about computers than my parents do.

13. I have read at least two Harry Potter books.

14. Summer is my favorite season.

15. I'm looking forward to having a great school year.

Ask your students: "What are some qualities that define you? If you were to collect a set of words and phrases that are *just like you,* what would be on your list?" Explain to students that they will be making a poem of sorts, based on the phrase "Just Like (student's first name)" and containing personal characteristics that are interesting or worth sharing. Show them your own sample and the student samples on page 27 to give them an idea of how it should look. (Kara's sample uses simpler vocabulary, while Josh's is more complex.)

3. Invite Students to Complete Their Own Responses

Have students come up with several common words and phrases that describe them and "upgrade" those words to more exotic synonyms using thesauruses or online resources. Thus, "nice" becomes "affable," and "brave" becomes "stouthearted." Here's an example:

Kind of well-ad**J**usted
ca**U**stic
addicted to beache**S**
Traveler

        Laid-back
        wr**i**ter
        Kinesthetically challenged
        easy cri**e**r

slow **J**ogger
philosoph**i**c
open-**m**inded

As you can see, students may select words and phrases that contain the letters of their name anywhere within them, not just at the beginning. This allows for more freedom and variation in their responses.

Consider having your students complete this activity working in small groups. Not only can students with stronger vocabularies help guide other students, but students who know one another well might be able to give each other suggestions about words or phrases that fit their interests or personalities.

As with the previous activities, you may wish to display the results next to a student's photo on a bulletin board that highlights four or five students a week, on the cover page of a student's personal website, or simply in front of the students' desks.

Extensions

Classroom Extensions

1. To include this activity as part of an autobiography, have students complete three separate sheets: "Just Like ___ Was," "Just Like ___ Is," and "Just Like ___ Will Be." These can be accompanied by brief essays that link the three aspects of one's life together: past, present, and future.

2. Instead of having students write their own "Just Like ___" responses, pair them up and have the two pupils interview one another, looking for clues as to what might be included on each other's "Just Like ___" sheet. After the students have completed one another's forms, get them back together to check how accurate the responses seem to be.

3. Using fictional characters or historical individuals the students have read about or studied, complete a "Just Like ___" sheet as part of a larger project on this person's life or accomplishments. Display a bulletin board connecting each character's or individual's "Just Like _____" poem with a drawing or other image of this individual.

School Extension

Get together with your grade-level or team teachers and complete a "Just Like ___" sheet using the name of the *school* instead of the name of an individual. For example, if your school is named "Chambers Middle School," then the "C" might stand for "<u>c</u>hild-centered," the "h" for "very long <u>h</u>allways," the "m" for "scru<u>m</u>ptious lunches," and so on. Use this during your orientation sessions with students, prior to or following the "That's Just Like Me!" activity in your classrooms.

Family Extension

On your classroom blog or website, or in your weekly or monthly newsletter to parents, share a few student responses to this activity, inviting families to sit down and do this lesson together using the family last name (or last names). Ask permission to print some of these family responses in upcoming editions of the blog, website, or newsletter so that both the kids and the parents get to know one another a little better throughout the year.

Just Like Me!
Sample Student Responses

Just Like Kara!

Jolly
fUn to be around
soft Spot for the underdog
Tries to do well

aLtruistic
eighth grader
loves thinKing
lots of quEstions

Kind
Always wandering
pRecise
black hAir

Just Like Josh!

nonJudgmental
Utilitarian
haplesS (sometimes)
Tempermental

Loquacious
whimsical
Knick's fan
Eerie

Jovial
Obstreperous
Sassy
Organizationally disHeveled

5. The Other Side of Me

Sometimes, the best activities are handed to us by students, as was the case when a young man named Les handed Jim a copy of *Skateboarding* Magazine. "Turn to the last page," he said, noting Jim's surprise. Something in a previous class of Jim's had convinced him that Jim would appreciate this article.

Titled "Last Words," this monthly feature provided an interview with a famous skateboarder. The 35+ questions included items such as these:

- What is the last book you read?

- When was the last time you felt out of place?

- When was the last time you felt afraid?

- When was the last time you felt cheated?

- When was the last time you felt loved?

Of course, less-enriching questions were included but, for the most part, the questions were probing, serious inquiries into the mind and life of somebody known for what he does well. So, Les, thank you for the magazine and for providing the seeds for an activity our students really enjoy.

Product	Students interview each other and create posters featuring the *back* of the interviewee's head with several thought bubbles describing the person
Materials	<ul><li>1 piece of poster board per student</li><li>Writing and drawing materials</li><li>1 copy of the "The Other Side of Me" interview questions handout (pages 31–32) per student</li><li>1 copy of the "The Other Side of Me" interview ground rules handout (page 33) per student</li><li>1 display copy of "The Other Side of Me" sample student response (page 34)</li></ul>
Time	Three 45-minute class sessions: the first one to introduce the activity and begin the interviews; the second to complete the interviews and check for accuracy of the information; and the third to create the poster
Common Core State Standards	Activity meets standards 2, 3, 4, 6, 12, 14, 15, and 16 from the chart on page 5.

Activity Steps

1. The Hook

Before you begin this activity, ask a colleague (preferably another teacher who knows your students) to participate in this hook with you. Even better would be if this colleague decides to involve his or her class in this project's completion.

Reserve the media center or any area large enough to seat all of your students on the floor for several minutes. You'll want them to be within earshot of the conversation between you and your colleague that will follow. Set up two chairs back-to-back.

As the students arrive, direct them to sit on the floor, close to where the chairs are set up. You and your colleague need a copy of "The Other Side of Me" interview questions and a pencil or pen to write down answers given by the other person. Sitting back-to-back, one teacher begins by asking any one of the questions on the sheet. As the other person answers, the question poser takes notes on the teacher's response. Then, it is the other person's turn to ask a question and record the answer. Continue this for at least seven questions each.

2. Introduce the Activity

After you've completed the hook step (usually it takes about 15 minutes), ask the students what was common about every question (they all asked about the last time you did something). Then, ask if they learned anything about these adults that they didn't know before. Do they have things in common with their teachers that they didn't know about? Things that make the teachers seem more interesting, human, likable, or admirable?

Tell students they will have the opportunity to ask these and other questions of a classmate who will be chosen at random, and their final product will be a poster of this individual, with a drawing of the *back* of his or her head. Why the back? Well . . . this activity is called "The Other Side of Me," and its purpose is to reveal interesting information about a person that he or she might not usually share—information from the person's private side. Show them the completed student sample so they can get an idea of what their final product might look like.

Distribute the interview questions sheet and the interview ground rules sheet. Review the ground rules together, noting especially that each person has the opportunity to "pass" on any question they feel uncomfortable answering.

Finally, randomly pair up students and get ready for the interviews to begin.

3. Invite Students to Complete Their Own Responses

Give students 20–30 minutes to interview each other, taking turns asking one question at a time. They should get answers for 7–10 questions during this time. Tell students to take notes that are complete enough that they will recall their partner's responses later, and reiterate that it is okay to ask for elaboration if they did not understand their partner's initial response. If they get enough answers before time is up, and if they would like to do so, let them know that they can make up one "when was the last time" question of their own to ask.

Although the two adults did not face each other during the questioning, we've found that it is just too distracting for some students to sit back-to-back. So, you may give students the option of facing each other, knee to knee.

Continue interviews on the next day of class. Make sure you reserve enough time for students to share their responses with their partner to check for accuracy of information. Students may add clarifying details to their responses at this point.

During the third class session, have students create the posters: They draw the back of their partner's head in the center of the poster and write or type their partner's responses to the questions on the outer two-thirds of the poster, placing each response inside its own talk balloon. Completed posters should carry the name of the subject of the poster on the front as well as the creator's name on the *back*.

Extensions

Classroom Extensions

1. Ask students to brainstorm additional questions that would be good to ask someone if you wanted to get to know that person better or, if any students already created some of their own questions during the activity, they can be added to this newly created list. Compile these questions onto a master list that you can later share with the class as journal prompts.

2. If you have student teachers in your school, ask them if they, as a group, would participate in answering "The Other Side of Me" questions. Several student representatives from your classroom can serve as interviewers/note-takers, and the responses (and the back-of-the-head posters) can be placed in a display case next to a *real* photograph of the student teachers. This can be a way to make the student teachers feel welcomed, as well as to introduce them to staff and students they might not meet otherwise.

3. To add a technological element to the activity, have students use the free online poster-making tool Glogster, at www.glogster.com. They can scan and upload their drawings and type question responses into word bubbles, and they can add other elements, such as graphics, photos, music, and video. All of the elements on their posters can be tweaked in many ways, such as color, shadow, tilt, shape, and size, and posters can be shared the same way a blog post can.

School Extension

At a faculty meeting, share "The Other Side of Me" handout with other teachers. Ask them to create new questions that relate more specifically to their roles as educators. For example, "When was the last time you had a lesson fail?"; "When was the last time you were proud to be a teacher?"; "When was the last time a student made you feel important in his or her life?"; "When was the last time you counted the days until the next school vacation?" Staff volunteers can then answer the questions raised by their colleagues as both fun and poignant ways to review the ups and downs of being a teacher.

Family Extension

Suggest families do this activity at home, with adults paired up with kids. The same ground rules apply about being able to say "pass" on a particular question. As an additional activity, kids can share the responses they got from their parents with their grandparents, making this an intergenerational sharing time that can be both enjoyable and revealing.

The Other Side of Me Interview Questions

1. What was the last book you started but did not finish?

   _____

   _____

2. What was the last award you received?

   _____

   _____

3. When was the last time you lost something?

   _____

   _____

4. What was the last movie you walked out on?

   _____

   _____

5. When was the last time you felt out of place?

   _____

   _____

6. When was the last time you felt truly happy?

   _____

   _____

7. When was the last time you were injured?

   _____

   _____

8. When was the last time you felt afraid?

   _____

   _____

9. When was the last time you felt respected?

   _____

   _____

10. When was the last time you failed?

    _____

    _____

11. When was the last time you felt embarrassed?

    _____

    _____

12. When was the last time you felt loved?

    _____

    _____

13. When was the last time you felt totally confused?

    _____

    _____

continued →

14. What was the last good advice you received?

_____

_____

15. What was the last memorable place you visited?

_____

_____

16. When was the last time you wanted to give up?

_____

_____

17. What was the last thing you celebrated?

_____

_____

18. What was your last nightmare?

_____

_____

19. Who was the last person who inspired you?

_____

_____

20. When was the last time you cried?

_____

_____

21. When was the last time you felt envious of someone?

_____

_____

22. When was the last time you laughed?

_____

_____

23. What was the last event that changed your life?

_____

_____

24. When was the last time you made somebody proud?

_____

_____

25. When was the last time you acted silly?

_____

_____

26. Who was the last person who made you feel special?

_____

_____

The Other Side of Me

INTERVIEW GROUND RULES

IN ORDER TO BE SURE EVERYONE HAS AN ENJOYABLE AND COMFORTABLE TIME CONDUCTING INTERVIEWS, PLEASE FOLLOW THESE RULES:

1 If you don't really know the person you are interviewing, you may talk with him or her for a couple of minutes to get acquainted before the interview.

2 Look over the questions that you are most interested in asking. Remember, you only need to get answers to 7–10 questions.

3 For each question you ask, record your partner's response in enough detail that you'll remember it later. You will use your notes to write a complete statement in a word bubble on the poster.

4 After your interviews are completed, share your notes with your partner so that she or he can correct or add details to the responses. You might even want your finished answers to be written in the first-person voice, as in Alec's sample response.

5 If you ask a question and your partner says, "pass," she or he does not have to answer that question. *Do not ask why she or he won't answer the question!* Simply move on to a different question.

6 Remember that you are taking turns answering and asking questions.

7 If you have any questions or concerns during this activity, please raise your hand and your teacher will help you.

The Other Side of Me
Sample Student Response

When was the last time you felt truly happy?
When my mom told me that even though our house finally sold, we were not going to be moving to another town. So, I'd be able to still hang around with all of my friends.

When was the last time you felt afraid?
Actually, it was two years ago when I was just beginning middle school. I was convinced that the eighth graders would reign terror on all of us little sixth graders. It didn't happen, though. Well, not very much.

What was the last book you started but did not finish?
My algebra textbook. I changed classes after a month because I had no idea what I was doing in this class. If it's supposed to be math, why use all those letters?

What was the last memorable place you visited?
My dad's new apartment in Indianapolis. It was nice, but it really wasn't "homey," if you know what I mean.

What was the last good advice someone gave you?
To continue my dream to become a comedy writer instead of something "important" like a doctor or lawyer. Most people laugh when I tell them my goal . . . this teacher didn't.

When was the last time you lost something?
Well, I was with my little brother at the mall and all of a sudden he wasn't there. As luck would have it, I found him in five minutes, before my mom ever knew he was gone. He was looking at this lady making pretzels.

When was the last time you felt loved?
It was a combination deal: my mom was watching my favorite TV show with me, my crazy cat was purring on my lap, and I was eating my favorite pizza. Ahhhhhh . . .

When was the last time you felt out of place?
Did you not notice my response about algebra class? Fish out of water? That was me!

(ALEC, 8TH GRADE)

6. Me in a Nutshell

Many people, when they visit a vacation destination for the first time, will research the place for sights to see, places to go, and not-to-be-missed highlights. They may scan the Internet for suggestions, but they may also use brochures and pamphlets issued by local attractions or the visitors' bureau.

In this activity, your students introduce themselves to others in a similar way—by producing a brochure about themselves. Unlike other activities in Section 1, "Me in a Nutshell" involves more extensive thought, work, and time from your students. The end result, though, can be more introspective, revealing, and satisfying responses.

Product	A tri-fold brochure about the student that can be shared with classmates and family members
Materials	• 1 copy of the "Me in a Nutshell" activity directions (page 38) per student • 1 display copy of the "Me in a Nutshell" sample student responses (page 39) • 1 copy of the "Me in a Nutshell" interview notes (pages 40–41) per student • 1 copy of the brochure template (pages 42–43) per student • Photographs supplied by students of themselves, their family members, their pets, and/or other important elements of their lives • Access to computers (at home/school) • A referee's whistle
Time	Allow at least two 45-minute periods of in-class time, one at the beginning of the activity and another after the students have collected all the information for their brochures. Also, expect that students will need at least an additional hour of out-of-class work to interview people for their brochure and another hour to compile the interview information into written form. The activity should take students no more than two weeks total.
Common Core State Standards	Activity meets standards 2, 3, 4, 6, 12, 14, 15, and 16 from the chart on page 5.

Activity Steps

1. The Hook

Prior to the students' entrance into your classroom, list these phrases on the board:

- *Pet peeves*
- *Hot and not*
- *My future*
- *Personal heroes*
- *Favorites*

When students arrive, ask them to get into groups of four or five for a series of "two-minute conversations." Here's how they work: you define a category (for example: "*Pet peeves* are little things that people do that drive you crazy"; "*Favorites* include everything from favorite food to favorite color to favorite sport or type of music"), and students speak in round-robin fashion, taking no more than 20 seconds each, naming their answers within their small groups. (Be prepared, this part of the activity tends to get noisy.)

Blow the whistle to begin, and blow it again to stop each conversation and begin the next topic. Continue doing this until you have covered all five categories.

Afterward, have the class reassemble as a whole and ask students to contribute any unusual or interesting responses that came up in their small groups. Record these on the board or a projected computer screen under each category name. If students seem particularly intrigued by any of the responses, ask the students who provided them to elaborate.

2. Introducing the Activity

Show the "Me in a Nutshell" student sample responses and explain to students that this is what they are going to make: a project that will encapsulate their lives, including parts of it that they do not remember . . . but others do. It even includes a section for them to make predictions about their futures. In sum, it is going to be a type of autobiography written in the form of a brochure—a personal brochure—that reveals their lives in a nutshell. Read all the panels of the brochure with your students and answer any questions they have before handing out the directions sheet.

3. Invite Students to Complete Their Personal Responses

Distribute copies of the "Me in a Nutshell" directions sheet, which includes a template, and go over it together with your class. Much of the information students will obtain comes from their own minds and memories, but point out to them that the "When I Was Small" category will require them to speak with family members (or others) who knew them as babies or toddlers. The "Personal Heroes" section can be done without speaking to the hero, but it can be made richer in content if students can get responses directly from that individual in person or electronically. If the personal hero is deceased or unavailable, suggest they speak with someone who knew that hero personally. Distribute the interview notes handout to students, asking them to compose any additional questions they may wish to ask.

Provide students with a project timeline no longer than two weeks total, with these benchmarks as a guideline. You may want to have students check in with you at each benchmark.

- **Within three days:** Write first drafts of the categories that do not need other people in order to complete them.
- **Within five days:** Interview people for the "Personal Hero" and "When I Was Small" sections.
- **Within seven days:** Exchange drafts with a classmate and offer each other revision suggestions on any parts that seem confusing or incomplete (if needed, students can ask the teacher for help revising).
- **Also within seven days:** Complete the art and collect photographs or other visuals needed.
- **Within ten days:** Compile all the material into the brochure design according to the template (or a different, teacher-approved design).

After students turn in their final brochures, devote a class period or an event to sharing them. One way to approach this is to invite students to preview their brochures in small groups of students with whom they feel comfortable before posting them on a wall or bulletin board. Do this as a celebration, with some type of snack and drink, so that the presentations seem less formal.

Many students enjoy sharing their personal brochures not only with friends and classmates, but also with other family members, especially grandparents or those who do not live close by. Encourage your students to distribute copies to important people in their lives, especially siblings away at college or grandparents who live elsewhere.

Note: Depending on the resources in your classroom and otherwise available to your students, you can have students produce their brochures by hand (by printing the template, handwriting responses, and pasting photos in place) or on the computer. This can be done without much trouble using a word processing program such as Microsoft Word or a design program such as InDesign. Ask a tech-savvy colleague or student for help if you are not sure how to approach this electronically.

Extensions

Classroom Extensions

1. One way to display these brochures months after they have been completed is to use them as the front and back covers of writing portfolios that students maintain throughout the year. These portfolios contain the students' best work samples of the year, all encased in either a scrapbook or three-ring binder. During the last few days of the school year, you may reserve space in the media center and set aside a time for parents, siblings, grandparents, and "personal heroes" selected by the students to come in and read some of the students' writing projects. Allot time for student volunteers to read one short writing sample, but the main emphasis is on small group, personal sharing. Of course, not all students have someone show up to review their portfolios, but if you invite your colleagues (teachers, custodians, counselors, secretaries), many will drop by and look through your students' portfolios. If you offer food, it's guaranteed to increase your audience size!

2. Have students build personal Web pages instead of printed brochures. Depending on your level of technical expertise, you can help them create their own designs to display the information on the "Me in a Nutshell" handout or simply have students use the brochure template. This option can help students get more feedback on their material, because it's easy to send a link to the URL using email or through your class newsletter. You can also get feedback using Twitter by asking teachers from other classes and schools to check out your students' work online and leave comments.

School Extensions

1. This activity is ideal for a team-wide or grade-level activity. After students complete their brochures, have classes visit each other and share their work in pairs or small groups.

2. Ask interested students who have completed their personal brochures to work with younger students who struggle to write. Or, connect with the special education teachers in your school to identify individual students who could benefit from the help of some of your more capable students in helping them create their own "Me in a Nutshell" brochures.

Family Extension

Invite students to compose a letter to the personal heroes they selected (or a friend or relative of the heroes). This letter can contain a detailed description as to why the student selected this individual as a hero. Mail or email this letter, along with a copy of the personal brochure, to the hero or selected family member.

Me in a Nutshell Activity Directions

A nutshell may be quite small, but within it is contained a whole lot of good eating and nourishment. When people talk about summarizing a topic "in a nutshell," they mean they are going to say a whole lot in a short amount of space and time. Sure, some parts will be left out, but the most important elements of the subject will be there for all to see.

Your life—past, present, future—is way bigger than can be contained by even the world's biggest nutshell, but in this activity, you're going to stuff as much information as possible about yourself and those you care about into a small amount of space. The final product will look something like a tourist brochure advertising an amusement park, but instead of giving information on the steepest water slide or fastest roller coaster, it's going to provide tidbits about you.

To complete your brochure, you'll need to write material for ten sections. Use the word count guidelines to make sure your text fits in the spaces allotted.

1. Me in a nutshell: This is an overall summary of who you are and what you like to do. Even though this category is mentioned first, it's probably best to complete it *last* so that you don't repeat a lot of what you wrote in the other categories.
•••••••••••••• **About 100 words.** ••••••••••••••

2. Little known facts: Are you related to someone famous? Can you twirl a baton on your nose? Have you visited Antarctica and danced with penguins? Make a list of five things about yourself that people might find surprising.
•••••••••• **Five items, one sentence each.** ••••••••••

3. Pet peeves: What small things do people do that drive you crazy? Fingernails on a chalkboard? Interrupting you whenever you speak? Here's the space to let it out.
•••••••••••••• **About 50 words.** ••••••••••••••

4. When I was small: You may think you know yourself, but others knew you *before* you knew yourself. Interview one or two people who remember you when you were much younger, ask them to describe what you were like, and write about what you learn.
•••••••••••••• **About 100 words.** ••••••••••••••

5. Free time: What do you enjoy doing when you don't have homework or chores at home to complete? Soccer? Texting? Painting your toenails different colors? Do tell.
•••••••••••••• **About 50 words.** ••••••••••••••

6. Favorites: Choose your own categories—food, sport, TV show, actor, video game, etc.—and name your favorite in each one.
•••••••••••••• **List 12 categories.** ••••••••••••••

7. Personal hero: Most everyone has heroes, and a lot of them aren't even famous. They are friends, relatives—even teachers. Select one person as your hero (someone you actually know) and tell why that person has played such a vital role in your life.
•••••••••••••• **About 100 words.** ••••••••••••••

8. Hot and not: Create a two-column list. On the "Hot" side, list things that *to you* are hot (fun, interesting, cool, delicious, beautiful, etc.), and on the "Not" side, list corresponding things that—in your opinion—most definitely are not. Use any categories you like, from music and fashion to video games and food.
•••••••••••• **Five items in each column.** ••••••••••••

9. The future: As you look ahead ten . . . fifteen . . . twenty years from now, where do you think life will take you? Create your own future, and tell your readers what they might expect when they meet you as an adult.
•••••••••••••• **About 100 words.** ••••••••••••••

10. Your favorite self-portrait and quote: Bring in a favorite photo of yourself (or take a new one) as well as a favorite quote you like. The quote could be from a famous person, a person you know, a song lyric, or a quote that you simply make up yourself. Be sure to type your name under your photograph.
••

Use the template provided to put together your brochure. Soon you will have your entire life encased in a metaphorical nutshell that introduces your readers to one very interesting individual: you.

Me in a Nutshell Sample Student Responses

Me in a nutshell

Seth: My name is Seth Lawrence. I'm a polite, outgoing, smart teenager. I've moved around multiple times but have pretty much spent my life around Harrisburg, Pennsylvania. I like building, designing, and fixing objects. If you were to sum me up, you'd say I'm short, talkative, and kind. And you'd never forget you'd met me.

Little known facts

Ebony: (1) I'm related to Daniel Boone. (2) I've never broken a bone. (3) I got lost in my backyard when I was four. (4) I've never been on an airplane. (5) I was named after an aunt I never met.

Pet peeves

Seth: I hate when people are talking and they spit all over you. Even if they don't mean it, it's still disgusting. And don't you hate it when people lick their fingers after eating chocolate? Yuck!

When I was small

Ebony: My mom says that when I was a toddler, I liked to go to the zoo and pull on people's coattails. Who knows why? She said I always loved to color, even when I was two and really just scribbling. The Hello Kitty lunchbox I pack my lunch in even today was a gift she gave me when I was in first grade. My kindergarten teacher described me as outgoing—a little too much, from what she told me.

Free time

Seth: Surprisingly, watching TV is not something I like to do. I'd rather read a book or draw something. Going outside is always fun because you can get away with things outside that you could *never* do inside.

Favorites

Ebony: *Favorite sports:* volleyball to play, pool (nine ball) to watch—really! *Favorite holiday:* Halloween (yay for costumes!). *Favorite food:* salad with raspberry vinaigrette. *Favorite month:* April, when the world turns green again.

Personal hero

Seth: My uncle Joe is so important to me. He has taught me numerous things, including how to be loose. He is president of his own company and lives in Dubai right now, but he's lived in many places (like me). He was a late bloomer and never a straight-A student, but look at him now! He has a great personality, and if you ever met him, you'd like him for sure.

Hot and not

Ebony: *Hot:* biking; *Not:* driving. *Hot:* being smart; *Not:* acting dumb. *Hot:* mismatched socks; *Not:* Velcro sneakers. *Hot:* Stephen King; *Not:* Stephenie Meyer. *Hot:* deep snow; *Not:* rain.

The future

Seth: I want to attend the University of North Carolina, because everything about the school excites me. I'd like to become an engineer or a scientist and, as an adult, I want people to see me as a smart, hardworking gentleman who knows how to have fun. I won't wait for the future to come to me, I'm reaching for it now.

Ebony: Oh gosh . . . the future! I wish I had more definite ideas about my place in it. College? Sure. Living in New York City? Maybe. Keeping the same job for 30 years? Never. I don't know if I'll ever marry, but how many 14-year-olds think they will? I want to travel, meet interesting people, and leave life knowing that I mattered to someone.

Favorite quote

Seth: "Change is just a breath away." (That's one of my original quotes.)

Ebony: "The truth is a beautiful and terrible thing and should be treated with great caution." (Albus Dumbledore, from *Harry Potter*)

Me in a Nutshell Interview Notes

As you prepare your "Me in a Nutshell" personal brochure, you will need to interview one or more people for the "When I Was Small" section and, if possible, the "Personal Hero" section. Use this sheet to prepare for your interview and take notes, and refer back to it when you write these sections.

When I Was Small

Name/relationship of the person interviewed:

_____

_____

What memories do you have of me as a young child?

Response:

_____

_____

_____

_____

_____

_____

_____

Were there particular things I liked to do or didn't like to do when I was small?

Response:

_____

_____

_____

_____

_____

_____

_____

_____

_____

_____

What three words best describe me as a young child?

Response:

_____

_____

_____

_____

_____

_____

_____

_____

_____

_____

(Make up your own question)

_____

_____

_____

Response:

_____

_____

_____

_____

_____

_____

_____

continued ➔

Me in a Nutshell Interview Notes (continued)

Personal Hero

Name/relationship of the person interviewed:

_____

Why do you think I chose you as my personal hero?

Response:

_____
_____
_____
_____
_____
_____

Of all the things you've done in life, what are a few of your proudest moments or greatest achievements?

Response:

_____
_____
_____
_____
_____
_____
_____
_____
_____
_____
_____
_____
_____

What were you like as a child?
What did you enjoy doing?

Response:

_____
_____
_____
_____
_____
_____
_____
_____
_____
_____
_____
_____

(Make up your own question)

_____
_____
_____

Response:

_____
_____
_____
_____
_____
_____
_____

Me in a Nutshell

Little Known Facts

Photo or Artwork

Free Time

Pet Peeves

When I Was Small

Favorites

Photo or Artwork

(Student name)

Photo of student completing this activity

Favorite Quote

Hot and Not

Photo or Artwork

The Future

Artwork or photo of personal hero

Personal Hero

Me in a Nutshell template side 2

Writing to Understand Ourselves

We believe the oft-quoted maxim that all writing is autobiographical. Even when the topic has nothing to do with yourself, how can you not infuse your written words with important elements from your life—the people and events that have shaped the person you've become, and thus your perspective on everything?

During the middle school years, when young adolescents have an increasing sense of self and desire for independence, writing can be a vital way for students to examine who they are and who they may become. Wise teachers take advantage of this mental energy, encouraging students to compose essays, poems, and songs in which the central theme is themselves. With honest and vivid language that erupts from the unfiltered thoughts and emotions so typical of this age, middle school students can compose meaningful, strong, evocative material that, like adolescence itself, makes you laugh one minute and cry the next.

Learning Objectives

- To encourage students to examine their lives for traces of insight and wisdom, and to record their findings in various written forms

- To provide students a forum to express their thoughts and opinions on questions that are personal, ethical, and/or philosophical in nature

- To use personal experiences to understand the complexities of life in areas such as personal and familial relationships, and to record these new understandings through prose, poetry, and music

- To provide peer audiences for students' written work, allowing discussion of some issues commonly faced by young adolescents

7. My Personal Quote Shield

We like to do this activity during the first month of the school year for three reasons. First, completing it involves both research and reflection, two skills students will need throughout the year. Second, its open-ended nature allows for students to make their responses as revealing or guarded as they feel comfortable. Lastly, the product itself makes a wonderful hall display, not only for staff and other students to see, but for parents and visitors to absorb as well.

Something else, too: By introducing students to a variety of worthwhile quotations, you give them access to the ideas of scientists, writers, artists, lyricists, and other figures whose wisdom transcends history and perches for a brief, timeless moment on the shoulders of the budding young authors in your classroom.

Product	Individually designed "shields" containing a favorite quote and an essay that explains the quote's importance to the student
Materials	• 1 sheet of colored construction paper per student (get many colors so students can choose) • 1 sheet of blank, unlined white paper per student • Lots of quotes; consider the websites www.quoteworld.org and www.thinkexist.com and the iPhone applications "Freequotes" and "Famousquotes" as sources • 1 display copy of a poem or lyrics to a song of your choosing that has a repeated chorus or verse (you can find lyrics at various websites, including www.songlyrics.com); if you use a song, consider playing it on a CD or MP3 player in class • 1 display copy of "Quotes of the Ages . . . Quotes from the Sages" (page 49) • 1 display copy of the personal quote shield student samples (pages 50–53)
Time	Three 45-minute class sessions, with a day or two in between each day for students to work on drafts of their essays
Common Core State Standards	Activity meets standards 2, 3, 4, 6, 12, 14, 15, 16, 18, and 19 from the chart on page 5.

Activity Steps

1. The Hook

As students enter your room and get settled, ask them to complete the following common expressions:

"To be or not to be . . ."
("that is the question." —Hamlet)

"Ask not what your country can do for you . . ."
("ask what you can do for your country."
—John F. Kennedy)

"Life is like a box of chocolates . . ."
("you never know what you're gonna get."
—Forrest Gump)

"The only thing we have to fear . . ."
("is fear itself." —Franklin D. Roosevelt)

Mention to your students that even though every one of these quotes comes from a much longer speech, movie, or play, people are able to recognize these one-liners almost immediately. "Such is the power of a well-turned phrase," you might add.

Next, play the song or read the poem you have selected that has a repeating chorus or verse. One of our favorites is from the rock group Green Day, titled "Good Riddance (Time of Your Life)." We play this short song and display its lyrics, which include this line repeated four times: "It's something unpredictable, but in the end it's right. I hope you had the time of your life." After listening to the song (or reading your selected poem), ask your students why you think its author chose to use the same line again and again. The most common response you're likely to receive? "The writer really wanted you to think about the message in these few words."

2. Introduce the Activity

Now that you've primed your students on how a short statement can leave a big impact, mention that this activity involves finding a quote that has personal relevance for them and writing an essay detailing why. They will type the quote onto a piece of paper (in large letters) that will be attached to a sheet of construction paper that will then be cut into the shape of a shield.

The shield has symbolic significance: In the Middle Ages, shields were used to both *identify* a particular clan and to *protect* the person holding it. In this activity, students will use this same symbolism: telling readers who they are and explaining why the selected quote is one that makes them feel comfortable, safe, or protected.

Show the two sample quote shields and read the quotes and essays together. Point out to your students that each essay is divided into two sections: the first section is just a short paragraph that gives the student's interpretation of the quote ("I think this quote means _____ because _____"). The second section explains the significance of the quote to the student's life. This is the format your students should follow.

To introduce your students to some quotes and how to interpret them, display the "Quotes of the Ages . . . Quotes from the Sages" page and discuss the quotes, asking students to interpret the meaning of each. (We selected quotes for student interest; however, not all of the people quoted are of flawless character.) Accept multiple interpretations, but ask students to explain how they arrived at the interpretations they did. If the individual quoted is not familiar to your students, you may want to provide a brief overview of the person's life and/or work.

3. Invite Students to Complete Their Own Responses

It's time for students to select quotes for their shields. Put a quote website up on your interactive white board; have students navigate to sites on their own computers, tablets, or smart phones; prepare handouts with collected quotes; or provide books of quotes, and have students begin searching. Most sources allow users to search for quotes by theme or by author. For most of your students, theme will be the most helpful way to go. (Hint: If you're using a quote website, check it out before class to figure out how to navigate it most efficiently—each site has thousands of quotes.)

By the end of the first period, your students should have found the quote they want to use and typed or printed it onto a sheet of paper. Students may want to take more time at home to find the right quote for them. Have them write the first draft of their essays at home, to be due in a couple of days.

At a subsequent class meeting, have students share their work with several classmates and provide each other with feedback, including specific revision ideas regarding clarity, word choice, interpretation of the quote, and relevance of the quote to the students' lives. You may want to have students work in small revision groups for the whole period or, if you have computers available, begin work on their revisions after brief workshop meetings.

The final, revised essay should be completed as homework and due in a third class period. On this final day of the activity, invite students to decorate their shields with colors or designs, place their revised essays on a sheet of paper beneath the decorated shield, and share their work with one another in small groups or with the entire class. The shields and essays can then be displayed in a school hallway or display case.

Extensions

Classroom Extensions

1. Once students have selected a quote and cited its author, have them do some investigative work as to who this person was or is. Does the person have additional quotes worth reading? When was he or she alive? Does the person's occupation seem to be inspiration for the quote, or does the quote seem more personal? You could have a class discussion about this extension, as students introduce their "quote authors" to their classmates.

2. Instead of using famous quotes, ask students to do a similar activity using song lyrics (school appropriate, of course!). You may not want to complete this entire activity again, as it will be too similar in format to the one just completed, but as an interesting Friday afternoon activity, selected students can play a particular song whose lyrics they find meaningful, explaining why the song is one they enjoy.

3. If your local high school offers a class in philosophy, contact its teacher to see if she or he can "lend" you several students to come to your classroom and critique the quotes and interpretations selected by your students.

School Extension

Ask for student volunteers to select appropriate quotes and add them to the weekly bulletin that is provided to teachers and staff, or to a class website. Not only can the quotes be shared in this way, the students can also share their interpretations of these quotes in an abbreviated format.

Family Extension

Invite your students' families to identify a quote that has meaning to all family members or to write an original quote that has similar power. These quotes (and the rationale behind their selection) can be posted on your classroom's website or sent home in your email newsletter.

Quotes of the Ages . . .
Quotes from the Sages

"You have brains in your head. You have feet in your shoes. You can steer yourself any direction you choose."
Dr. Seuss, author

"You miss 100 percent of the shots you never take."
Wayne Gretzky, hall of fame NHL player

"No person is your friend who demands your silence or denies your right to grow."
Alice Walker, author

"The respect of others' rights, is peace."
Benito Juárez, former president of Mexico

"Be yourself 'cause everyone else is already taken."
Selena Gomez, actress

"Excellence is not a singular quality act but a habit. You are what you do repeatedly."
Shaquille O'Neal, athlete

"I don't know the key to success, but the key to failure is trying to please everybody."
Bill Cosby, comedian

"Dreams become reality when we put our minds to it."
Queen Latifah, actress and singer

"When I was growing up, I always wanted to be somebody, but now I see that I should have been more specific."
Lily Tomlin, comedian

"My mom is always telling me it takes a long time to get to the top, but a short time to get to the bottom."
Miley Cyrus, actress and singer

"I'm just trying to change the world one sequin at a time."
Lady Gaga, singer

"The truth is you don't know what is going to happen tomorrow. Life is a crazy ride, and nothing is guaranteed."
Eminem, rapper and actor

"I think the thing to do is enjoy the ride while you're on it."
Johnny Depp, actor

My Personal Quote Shield
Student Sample, *Lori, 8th grade*

Someone once asked me, "Why do you insist on taking the hard road?" and I replied, "Why do you assume I see two roads?"
— Anonymous

continued →

My Personal Quote Shield

Student Sample, *Lori, 8th grade* (continued)

This quote is about how some people take the easy way out of everything that comes their way. There is a saying that there is always another way to do something. Sometimes, though, there is not. Other times, your own integrity will not allow you to do anything other than the most difficult thing possible. These times come more often for some people than others, but we all reach a point in life when one occurs for us. Some people, myself included, can sometimes not allow themselves to take the easy way out because you would hate yourself if you did. It would hurt you to do anything other than your best. That is the reason this quote is so meaningful to me.

Perfect example: I was making a project for a class. It could have been done very easily. I could have done a sloppy job and just turned in anything and I still would have had a high grade because my percentage was already so high. Yet I couldn't allow myself to do the easy thing. I worked incredibly hard to make sure that my writing and presentation were the best they could be. Quality work earned me a quality grade.

I was proud of that grade and what it represented. My friends were amazed that I would go to so much trouble just for a project. I couldn't explain it to them, but my conscience was satisfied and my inner honesty to myself was intact.

My Personal Quote Shield

Student Sample, *Cody, 7th grade*

Do not dwell in the past, do not dream of the future, concentrate the mind on the present moment.

Siddhartha Gautama

continued →

My Personal Quote Shield

Student Sample, *Cody, 7th grade* (continued)

To me, this quote simply means that you can mope over mistakes in the past, or look ahead to a different future as much as you want. However, moping won't change the past and fantasizing won't prepare your future. You have to concentrate on what is going on in the present if you want to succeed in anything you do.

I've made mistakes in my past. Things could have been different if I hadn't made them. For example, from the moment I was born I couldn't see out of one eye. I wasn't completely blind, but the vision out of my left eye was so bad I may as well have been blind. It wasn't until late in my kindergarten year that I told my parents about my condition. When my mom asked why I hadn't told her earlier, I told her it was because I didn't want to wear glasses. Even though my vision has improved, it still isn't great. If my bad vision would have been caught sooner, it would be a whole lot better now. Still, dwelling on the past isn't going to change the present, so I moved on.

I often dream and worry about the future. About things like whether I'll get decent grades in high school, and if I'll be able to get into college (or afford it, for that matter). I worry if I'll get a good job and make it in the "real world." So, even though I could write a 500-word essay on how my life could turn out, the only thing that I have control over is how I live my life today, which is why I like this quote so much. It backs up my personal beliefs.

8. The Pyramid of Personal Qualities

All of our kids have hopes and dreams about their futures, but they are often much better at articulating their goals than they are at figuring out how to accomplish them. For example, someone does not become a successful writer or athlete by simply wishing it so, and not many people reach Nirvana by merely getting in the car, driving west, and turning left at Sacramento. Instead, most successful and happy people have gotten there through hard work, dedication, creativity, passion, or any number of other personal qualities.

This activity is designed to help your students consider not only their goals, but also the underlying personal attributes it takes to reach one's dreams.

Product	Two- or three-dimensional pyramids that list qualities students have now—and will have in the future—that help them attain their self-set goals; the pyramids are accompanied by brief, written explanations from the students highlighting the merits of these qualities
Materials	• 1 sheet of construction paper (for two-dimensional pyramids) or 1 sheet of poster board (for three-dimensional pyramids) for each student • 1 sheet of blank, white paper for each student • 1 copy of the "Poems to Ponder" handout (page 57) per student • 1 display copy of "The Pyramid of Personal Qualities" student samples (pages 58–59)
Time	Two 45-minute periods in class, or one 45-minute period with the students' final drafts assigned as homework
Common Core State Standards	Activity meets standards 2, 3, 4, 6, 12, 14, 15, 16, 17, 18, and 19 from the chart on page 5.

Activity Steps

1. The Hook

Before students arrive to class, display the following jumbled words on the board (do not include the solutions in parentheses):

    pohe (hope)

    eprcset (respect)

    sisterpecen (persistence)

    rugcoae (courage)

    reaf (fear)

    nisosap (passion)

    enohtys (honesty)

Ask your students to decipher the words, writing their answers next to the scrambled words.

After the words are decoded, ask for volunteers to talk briefly about specific experiences they've had with any of these. Perhaps a student will cite the persistence needed to pass Algebra 2; another may relate how hope was important in trying out for the lead in the class play; a third student might mention courage in standing up for a classmate being bullied. After a few examples are given, mention that not only do these qualities come into play day-by-day, they may also guide us toward reaching our present and future goals. Say: "Let's see these qualities in action."

2. Introduce the Activity

At this point, distribute the "Poems to Ponder" handout, telling students that each one of the seven poems describes one of the terms on the word list (the list is printed on the bottom of the "Poems to Ponder" page.) It is their job to determine which word best fits with which poem.

Have students work on this activity individually, mentioning that they will have a chance in a few minutes to compare their answers with those of their classmates. What they don't know is that there are no right or wrong answers for this activity. Indeed, what requires courage for one person to overcome can be another person's passion, and what gives one individual fear might give another hope. Explain to the students that each word can be used only once, so it might be best to read all seven poems before responding to any of them.

Once the students begin, several will likely question whether this activity really *has* right answers. After about five minutes, have a class discussion about the answers. Read aloud each poem, and ask for volunteers to say which term goes with it—and defend the reasons for their choices. In response, say something like, "That sounds right" or "I can see why you answered that way" *to every response your students provide.*

Of course, this will drive your students crazy, as they are conditioned to want to know which answer is *the* answer. You can tell them what many will have realized already: the right answers to this activity depend entirely on the personal perspective of the individual completing it. Ask them how this can happen in everyday life: you may see things totally different from someone else. Define "perspective" for them.

Now that you have your students either confused or irate, tell them the purpose of the activity: to get them thinking about personal qualities, especially qualities that are important to them. These qualities that play important roles in helping students reach their goals might be academic ("getting better grades"), social ("making friends with older kids"), or future-focused ("getting into Ohio State"). Whatever these individual goals might be, an examination of the personal qualities needed to attain them is an exercise worth exploring. That's where the pyramids come in.

Note: This activity is not meant to focus on any specific goal or goals of students, but rather on their goals in general—the person they want to become.

Display the two student samples, and ask your students if any of the words on the pyramids are unfamiliar to them; if so, explain their meanings. After the students have read the student essays explaining their word choices, tell them that even though all of these qualities were important to the students who wrote them, the *most* important quality is the one at the base of the pyramid. Those qualities are a foundation for the other qualities. The remaining four qualities are also vital to the students, but as they get higher on the pyramid they get smaller—and accordingly less important.

3. Invite Students to Complete Their Own Responses

By now, your students will have figured out their task: to come up with their own "Pyramid of Personal Qualities," which should include five personal qualities along with a one- to three-sentence explanation for each. Your students may find a thesaurus (in print or online) a handy tool in locating some other qualities, or you can brainstorm together a list of other qualities to get your students started.

You may allow your students to choose whether to create a two-dimensional pyramid or a three-dimensional one, or you may require one or the other. Students who create two-dimensional pyramids simply choose a piece of construction paper and cut it into a triangle; the explanations can be typed and placed below the pyramid (as on the samples). For three-dimensional pyramids, have students cut out four identical triangular shapes. On one of these sides, have them list the words, and have them type their explanations on the other faces. When completed, they should tape the poster board pieces together from the inside.

Extensions

Classroom Extensions

1. Use this activity to examine a main character in a book the students are reading by having students create a pyramid for this character. For example, in an eighth-grade class that was reading S.E. Hinton's *The Outsiders*, one student wrote about Ponyboy Curtis: "He has *passion* because he loves to read and write and his emotions are always easy to notice. He has *hope* because he likes to watch sunsets and daydream. And every day, he *perseveres* to get through life's simplest problems."

2. Ask your students to select an occupation that interests them and determine what attributes it takes to be successful in this career. Have students contact someone who is employed in this career, sharing the list of attributes, and asking this professional to add other attributes she or he considers helpful in preparing to enter this profession.

School Extension

Ask volunteers from your class to conduct a schoolwide (or grade-level) poll of students, asking the following questions:

- In choosing a friend, what qualities do you consider most important?
- What qualities do your best teachers possess?
- Are certain qualities essential for everyone to have?

The results of these polls can be posted on large paper and hung in the cafeteria or read during morning announcements.

Family Extension

After your students have completed this activity, compile a list of all the qualities that were selected and send this roster home to families. Tell the parents the nature of this activity and ask them to return the list to you with five items circled—the five attributes that they perceive as the most important ones to become a successful, responsible adult. Share these results with your students so they can compare this list with the qualities they had chosen earlier.

Poems to Ponder

Read each short verse and then, using the word choices below,
select which word you believe best fits each verse.

1

Saying "yes, and I mean it"
And "no" when I don't
While never confusing
"I will" with "I won't."

_____

2

The edge of a cliff,
The brink of a tear,
A ghost in the closet
with no one else near

_____

3

Baseball in April,
A rosebud in May,
A smile on your face
To begin every day.

_____

4

Being open to change
Standing tall by a friend,
Staying true to one's heart
From beginning to end.

_____

5

Believing in something
So hard that it stings.
Holding onto a dream
Until it grows wings.

_____

6

A fist, not a palm,
A frown, not a grin.
An attitude, a look
That lets no one else in.

_____

7

Truth, yes, but kindness, too.
Looking up to one's elders who are wiser than you.
Earning a medal the old-fashioned way,
Giving someone a lift at the end of the day.

_____

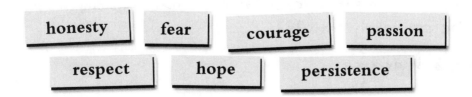

honesty   fear   courage   passion

respect   hope   persistence

The Pyramid of Personal Qualities
Student Samples

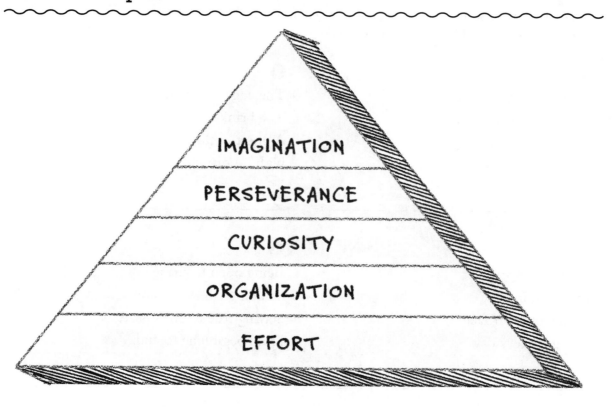

IMAGINATION: I like to dream of faraway places and someday going to them. I sometimes wish I was older, so I could explore the world. But then I think of how much fun it is to be young.

PERSEVERANCE: I don't quit at something just because I'm not good at it or mess up the first time. I keep pursuing my goal and trying to accomplish it.

CURIOSITY: I am always curious about how things work and how they came to be. I like facts and am curious how that fact became a fact.

ORGANIZATION: I like to organize things in and out of school. It makes me feel like I'm on top of things and being responsible. Organization makes things easier.

EFFORT: I think in order for me to accomplish something to the best of my ability, I have to put some effort into what I'm doing. I have to try hard to be completely satisfied.

— Brian, 8th grade

continued →

The Pyramid of Personal Qualities

Student Samples (continued)

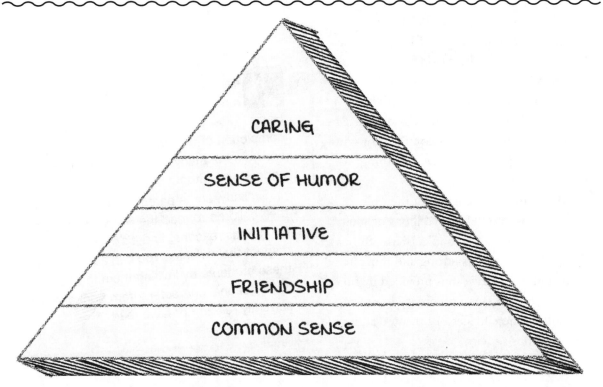

CARING

SENSE OF HUMOR

INITIATIVE

FRIENDSHIP

COMMON SENSE

CARING: If you are not kind to others, why should anyone be kind to you? It's not hard to smile or say "Hi," and doing it might actually make someone's day. Caring is definitely something I want on my list of "must-have" personal qualities.

SENSE OF HUMOR: Life is too serious as it is. Occasionally, you need a good laugh to keep yourself going.

INITIATIVE: Initiative is important because if you don't have it, you will never get anything accomplished. You need reasons to do things, and initiative gives you that. If you always put things off, your life will be harder.

FRIENDSHIP: Without friendship, I would lead a sad, lonely life with no point to it. All of us need someone to talk to, to laugh with, and to cry with. Without the quality of friendship, all of your feelings would have to be kept inside.

COMMON SENSE: This is the most important quality of all, for many reasons. One reason is because if you lack common sense, bad things will hurt you or get you in trouble. If that happens, you could lose things like friends or respect, or do badly in school.

— Monica, 7th grade

9. Lessons from Hogwarts

One has to wonder if J.K. Rowling ever anticipated that her series of Harry Potter books would take the world by storm the way they did. With more than 25 rejections for her first book, *Harry Potter and the Philosopher's Stone*, Rowling was told that her books were too long and complex for young readers. We guess this shows one thing: children notice quality.

Of course, children are not the only people hooked on Harry. Millions of adults (including us) find the books rich with compelling characters, strong and intricate plots, and great life lessons provided by the mentors, teachers, and others at Hogwarts School. It's these life lessons that are at the center of this activity.

Note: Although it is helpful if students have read at least one of the Harry Potter books, it is not essential for completion of this activity. The meaning and value of many of the quotes can be understood without context.

Similarly, some parents may not wish for their children to read the Harry Potter books, for various reasons, and it's important to respect their wishes. You can accommodate these students by inviting them to select other fictional characters from books they are currently reading or have read.

Product	Illustrated essays (300–400 words) based on a quote from a Harry Potter character that applies to students' own lives
Materials	• 1 display copy of the completed student sample "Lessons from Hogwarts" essay • 1 display copy of a summary of the main Harry Potter characters created by students in your class who know the books (or found online at websites such as "Top 25 Harry Potter Characters," movies.ign.com/articles/100/1002569p1.html) • Paper for printing or handwriting essays • Drawing supplies • 1 copy of a collection of quotes from the Harry Potter series for each student (compiled by you before class) or access to websites whose content is quotes from the books, including www.quotegarden.com/bk-hp.html
Time	Two 45-minute class periods with enough days in between for students to work on their essays and illustrations
Common Core State Standards	Activity meets standards 1–6, 10, 12, 14, 15, and 16 from the chart on page 5.

Activity Steps

1. The Hook

A day or two before you begin this activity, tell your students that you will be asking those who know the Harry Potter books to say something about their favorite plotlines and characters. Or, to increase the excitement, you could even do what many booksellers did prior to the release dates of most Potter books: post a countdown calendar that says "6 days to Potter . . . 5 days to Potter," and so on, tearing off another page each day.

When the day comes for the lesson to begin, show a short clip (five minutes at most) from the first Harry Potter movie, *Harry Potter and the Sorcerer's Stone*. (We suggest a segment with the students' early arrival at Hogwarts, which will include most of the main characters.)

Afterward, ask for volunteers to describe the main characters in the books. Of course, each book introduces new characters, and some of the characters are villainous in one book and chivalrous in another, but a general character summary is sufficient for now. If you can project your computer screen, or if you have an interactive white board, you can type notes as the discussion progresses to create a master sheet of character capsules. Alternatively, consider displaying the website "Top 25 Harry Potter Characters" on your white board or screen. This page provides summaries of the 25 most important characters in the series.

Make your character capsules available to students as an electronic file or provide them the website address, so they can refer to these as they work on their projects.

2. Introduce the Activity

At this point, distribute copies of the quotation handout you compiled or direct your students to a website that contains quotes from the series. Tell your students: One of the great strengths of the Harry Potter series is the sharing of wise and valuable lessons through the characters' conversations. Many of the books' greatest moments of insight are found in the dialog. A couple of examples include:

> *"If you want to know what a man's like, take a good look at how he treats his inferiors, not his equals."*
> —Sirius Black

> *"Have you any idea how much tyrants fear the people they oppress?"*
> —Albus Dumbledore

> *"There are all kinds of courage. It takes a great deal of courage to stand up to our enemies, but just as much to stand up to our friends."*
> —Albus Dumbledore

Divide students into small groups to discuss the quotes (try to include at least one student per group who knows the books well). Some of the quotes may seem straightforward in meaning, while others may be more complex or oblique. After about 15 minutes, ask for volunteers to read a selected quote and explain how they or their group interpret what the quote means. If other groups have selected the same quote, have the students identify ways their interpretations differ.

You don't need to review with your students every quote you've compiled. Instead, explain to students what their assignment is: They are going to write an illustrated essay that explains how a quote from the Harry Potter series (or the alternative book) connects to their own lives. Essays should be about 300–400 words (you may want to adjust the length requirement based on the needs and abilities of your students).

Show them the completed student sample and read it together. Point out how the essay is made up of two main parts:

1. An introduction of the quote and brief discussion of what it means.

2. A brief discussion of how the quote relates to the writer's life.

The illustration students complete may be of a concrete nature (for example, one of the Hogwarts buildings) or more abstract, representing something in the student's essay (for example, an ocean scene to represent life's constant changes, or a dry tree branch in a winter scene to represent coldness or despair).

3. Invite Students to Complete Their Own Responses

After looking at the student sample and discussing the assignment's parameters, give your students time in class to select their quotes and begin their essays. If students wish to find quotes other than the ones you provided, they may go to one of the many Harry Potter–related websites that list quotes from the book series.

Give students about a week to work on their essays and illustrations at home. On the day they're due, you may have students share their final essays in small groups, perhaps putting students together who chose the same quote or same character. Have the groups report to the class with thoughts about how their essays differed and were similar.

Display the essays on a large wall, where the particular quotes chosen are typed in large print on separate pages. This will attract the attention of passers-by, who might get curious to read the essays after being attracted by the quote. Another option, of course, is to post the essays and artwork to a class website or blog.

Note: For students who do not know the Harry Potter characters well, consider offering them the option of choosing a quote from a fictional character in another book with which they are more familiar. Another alternative would be for students to relate a Harry Potter quote to another book. For example, the quote from Albus Dumbledore that reads "Have you any idea how much tyrants fear the people they oppress?" could apply to the protagonists in The Bridge to Tarabithia, both of whom are bullied mercilessly in the early portion of the book. This option can be useful in sharing with students the universality of some human emotions and attributes, even in fictional characters.

Classroom Extensions

1. Make the reading of these activities a much bigger deal by inviting students to dress as their favorite Potter character as they present their essays to their classmates. Be sure to remind students that the underlying purpose of this lesson is to see how fictional characters' lives relate to their own, so they should focus on this as they explain the significance of their selected quote—not just the character who said it.

2. Ask students to select a favorite Harry Potter book (or another fiction book) and review no more than five pages of this book, looking for one quote or line of text that grabs their attention or makes them think. Have them discuss this quote in a journal entry, or orally with the entire class. The point? Good authors can cause others to think or feel something on almost every page of their books.

3. Harry Potter is not the only series of books that have attracted much student attention over the past few years. Certainly, the Chronicles of Narnia, the Lord of the Rings, the Twilight series, and others have garnered enthusiastic support from young readers as well. For students (and teachers) ready for a longer-term challenge, compare the plots, themes, and character development across these (or other) series of books and create a display board or other visual that reviews the commonalities and distinctions.

School Extension

Although many educators are aware of the Harry Potter books, few are as familiar with them as are their students. Hold a series of student-faculty dialogues about these books at which students introduce interested teachers to the books and their characters. It can begin with the basics—the characters and overall plots of the books—and can then graduate into more in-depth discussions of the underlying themes that relate to issues of growing up. Weekly or semimonthly get-togethers during advisory group time, lunch breaks, or even a "book club" are all options to consider. Be sure to engage a librarian in these presentations.

Family Extension

Invite parents and students to an evening event at which students introduce adults to the reasons the Potter books are so popular. Students can read their essays from this activity, or they can simply find other ways to explain the attraction of these books. Invite a young adult librarian to serve as the emcee, or request the same services from parents who have read the Harry Potter books with their children and can offer additional insights into their popularity.

Lessons from Hogwarts

Student Sample, *Lawrence, 8th grade*

In *Harry Potter and the Deathly Hallows*, the final book in the series, is a quote spoken by Albus Dumbledore: "Do not pity the dead, Harry. Pity the living, and above all, those who cannot love." J.K. Rowling has said that some of the main themes in her series are love and death. If this is so, then I believe this quote sums up the series.

In all of life's struggles, love is the all-consuming force that pushes us onward and keeps us from losing our own personal battles. Dumbledore says we should pity people who can't feel this powerful, positive emotion. Death is ultimately the end of this journey; it is the eternal respite from pain.

My grandfather died when I was very young, but still, I remember him every day. I no longer mourn his passing; he is happier than I can ever imagine. The fact that he is missed shows the power of love. Think of what a human is: just a piece of living, breathing flesh. But throw love into the equation and that human being becomes a father, a mother, a husband, a wife. He or she becomes much more than a human; love makes him or her immortal. Love creates life, but does death truly end life? Is someone really dead if they are loved?

I believe in a different cycle: love creates life, while death immortalizes that same life. There is no such thing as "movin' on."

I still wish my grandfather was in my life but, in some ways, I will always hold onto him. You don't need to be a Christian, or a Hindu, or even a wizard to believe this; you need only the love in your heart to accept it.

10. It Gives Me . . .

Jim created this activity as he thought about how to celebrate the last day of school with his students. Having spent two years together in a gifted program, Jim and his students had become closely bonded. The kids reminded Jim when he'd told the same joke once too often, and Jim had become expert in spotting those who looked thoroughly engrossed in his lesson when they were actually sneaking a listen to their hidden iPod.

The final day of school, especially when the students will be moving on to a different school the following year, is always a bittersweet moment of parting. Jim wanted a small remembrance of these rich two years, but time was short and students' willingness to write decreased as summer approached. But this activity, which is brief, comfortable, and reflective, is a great way to inspire sensitive, honest responses.

Product	A four-column collection of statements encapsulating each student's thoughts on his or her past, present, and future
Materials	• 1 copy of the "It Gives Me . . ." handout (page 67) per student • 1 display copy of the completed student samples "It Gives Me . . ." sheet (page 68) • Pencils or pens
Time	One 20-minute block of time for writing the assignment and then sharing it immediately with class members
Common Core State Standards	Activity meets standards 12, 14, 15, and 16 from the chart on page 5.

Activity Steps

1. The Hook

Say something to your students about whatever emotions you have about the end of the school year: the **joy** of knowing that you can sleep in for the next two months; the **anticipation** you feel at a summer full of outdoor adventures; the **relief** that accompanies not having to grade any more papers; and the **pang** of knowing that never again, after today, will "our class" be "our class."

Ask if any of your students have particular emotions today—the **ecstasy** of another year behind them, the **nervousness** of moving on to high school, the **trepidation** of not knowing what their final report card will have on it, etc.

2. Introduce the Activity

When student responses ebb, distribute copies of the "It Gives Me . . ." handout facedown, instructing students not to turn over the paper until everyone has one. Then, on the count of three, have students turn over the page, revealing the four categories: **Joy, Hope, Pride,** and **Pause**.

With the exception of "Pause," the other categories should be self-explanatory. Tell students that the phrase "It gives me pause" means something like "It causes me to stop and think," or, in some cases, "It causes me to worry." (For example, "It gives me pause to think about what I'll be doing in ten years" or "It gives me pause when I think about how much food is wasted in restaurants.")

3. Invite Students to Complete Their Own Responses

Direct students to quietly fill in at least four items for each category on their sheets. After about 10–15 minutes, while students are still working, walk around the room and select individual students to read one of their responses to whichever prompt you request. For example, as you walk by Laquisha, say "It gives me joy," and Laquisha answers with one of her statements. Then, move on to Ben and say, "It gives me pause," inviting him to say one of his answers. Continue this sharing until every student has had at least one chance to respond.

Next, return to the front of the room and begin saying the prompts randomly, asking anyone who wants to contribute to do so. Do this until the responses begin to diminish.

Generally, at the end of this activity, even the most rambunctious middle schoolers are calm and ready to reflect on your final question: "Why did I have you complete this assignment?"

Expect a couple of "You know . . . I wondered the same thing" comments, followed by some more sincere, thoughtful observations: "To show you what is important to us," "To think about where we've been and where we're going," or "To prove to us that our minds are always racing with random thoughts."

End the activity with a thankful tribute for a year (or more) well spent and an invitation to your students to return to middle school someday to share with you how they've grown.

Extensions

Classroom Extensions

1. Although we have found the most success doing this activity at the end of the year, it could be done at other times. You might combine it with "Me in a Nutshell," where family members who come to school to review students' writing portfolios complete it as a group. Then, responses are shared round-robin, one answer by a child, followed by one from an adult.

2. If your students read the same book together as a class, and there are complex characters in it, you could adapt this activity by having students complete the "It Gives Me . . ." handout from the point of view of one of the book's characters. In small groups, students who select the same character can share their responses and the reasoning behind them.

3. If your students read biographies throughout the year, ask them to complete the "It Gives Me . . ." handout from the point of view of the famous person they selected. For example, after reading about the fabled career of Hank Aaron, the student who read the biography could explain something about his life's triumphs and struggles on the "It Gives Me . . ." sheet. Just imagine how important figures like Georgia O'Keeffe, John F. Kennedy, Martin Luther King Jr., Sally Ride, or Marco Polo would respond to the topics of joy, pride, hope, and pause!

School Extension

During one advisory session, ask students to provide "It gives me . . ." responses out loud, which you, as the teacher, copy down. After doing so, read the responses back to the students and have them select the two or three responses that they believe are the most unique, awesome, inspiring, funny, or thoughtful. These can be read during the daily announcements or added to an ever-growing bulletin board in a prominent school location.

Family Extension

Invite your students' families to complete "It Gives Me . . ." sheets at home, including siblings, parents, grandparents, etc. In collecting each response, record the age of the person who gave it. Your students can then compile a chart of answers by age ranges (5–10; 11–19; 20–40; 41–60; 61+). You can also have students write their interpretations of how the depth and range of responses varies according to age, as well as what issues are common to all or most age ranges.

It Gives Me . . .

Joy

_____
_____
_____
_____
_____
_____
_____
_____
_____
_____
_____
_____
_____

Hope

_____
_____
_____
_____
_____
_____
_____
_____
_____
_____
_____
_____
_____

Pride

_____
_____
_____
_____
_____
_____
_____
_____
_____
_____
_____
_____
_____
_____
_____

Pause

_____
_____
_____
_____
_____
_____
_____
_____
_____
_____
_____
_____
_____
_____
_____

Student's Name:

_____

It Gives Me . . .

Sample Responses from Eighth Graders

Joy

- when I make babies laugh
- when girls come up behind me and put their hands over my eyes and make me guess who it is
- when I finish a good book and see the world from the eyes of a character in it
- when people give me the kindness I deserve rather than treating me as if I am not popular
- when I read Maya Angelou's poem "Phenomenal Woman"
- when I hear preschoolers singing their ABCs
- when my brother gives me a ride to school happily, with no complaints
- when I wake up on a summer morning, greeted by the sun, and realize that this day has the potential to be the best one of my life

Hope

- when I see a friend succeed in something I helped her learn
- when I think of my parents still being alive when I am an adult
- when I see a very biased person change his mind
- when I see my mother going through so much and still being strong and never hanging her head in shame
- when I see my grandmother and she still remembers who I am
- when I know I can talk to my sister about anything
- when my mom says "see you later" instead of "good-bye"

Pride

- when I understand something I have been struggling with
- when my sister dances
- when my favorite team, the Chicago White Sox, wins a game
- when I finally learn to do a trick on my skateboard that I've been practicing for weeks
- when I act like the good person that I am
- when I represent well my family, school, or town
- when I get treated like the young adult I will soon become

Pause

- when I think about the universe and my place in it
- when I lose my homework
- when I look at the world's problems and wonder how I can change them
- when I think about how fast my life is flying by—I'm 13 already!
- when I think that one day the world will be in my generation's hands
- when I think of a million questions that have no answers
- when I consider how many people struggle with something that is easy for me
- when I think about how happy I am with myself; it's actually quite remarkable!

11. Telling Your Own Story

The teachers we remember the most fondly and vividly are the ones who let us know that they, like us, had lives beyond school. We didn't need teachers to be our friends, but we did enjoy when our teachers spoke about movies they'd seen, vacations they'd taken, or the antics of their kids or pets. Education is among the most personal of professions; wise teachers know this and take advantage of it to enhance the education of their students.

Every student, whatever his or her particular life circumstances, has a story to tell that can *only* be told by that student. We realize that life doles out benefits unevenly, but all students share common denominators such as family, dreams, loss, and triumph. One student's annual vacation might include Paris and Rome, while the student sitting two rows over might be lucky to get to the local amusement park, but the personal stories that each of these students can tell about their life experiences can be equally as compelling.

That's what this lesson is designed to do: allow students to tell a story about their lives that no one else can tell better, because the students themselves are the central character in this real-life play. To impress on students the legitimacy of their stories, we always encourage them to submit their essays for publication in youth journals.

Product	A 500- to 700-word essay describing a person who was not in the student's life initially, became a part of the student's life, and then left (or changed dramatically)
Materials	• 1 copy of "Roger and Jim" (pages 73–74) for each student • Optional: 1 display copy of "Thankful for a Thanksgiving Change" (page 75) • Optional: 1 display copy of "My Gygy" (page 76) • Several sample copies of the journals *Creative Kids* or *Teen Ink* (both are hard copy journals but have portions available for free online at www.prufrock.com and www.teenink.com, respectively) • Authors' Guidelines for *Creative Kids* and/or *Teen Ink,* available at their websites • Optional: 1 display copy of "Yes, Middle Schoolers *Can* Write This Well!" (page 77)
Time	Two 45-minute class periods plus a homework assignment to revise and complete the final essay
Common Core State Standards	Activity meets standards 1–4, 6–8, 12, 14, 15, 16, and 19 from the chart on page 5.

Activity Steps

1. The Hook

Tell your students that they are about to read the story "Roger and Jim" about a 23-year-old man and his 14-year-old son. Now . . . if *that* doesn't grab the attention of your students, we don't know what will! They'll do the math in their heads, determining that it is biologically impossible for a man to become a father at the age of nine.

But under particular circumstances, like the ones explained in "Roger and Jim," such a situation is possible—in fact, the "Jim" in this instance is one of the authors of this book and Roger was his teenage foster son for almost a year and a half. No need to tell your students this, since they will discover it for themselves as they read the short story.

2. Introduce the Activity

As you distribute "Roger and Jim" to students, ask them to read it to themselves (this should take about 15 minutes). Upon completion, place the students into small groups, asking them to select the parts of the story they found most interesting and the writing techniques they thought were effective. Also, ask them to choose any parts of the story that were confusing or any writing techniques they didn't like.

Students may comment that they found the story to be sad, and many may have questions about what happened to Roger after this story ends. They may comment on the vocabulary that allows the reader to almost see or hear what the author is experiencing—for example, Roger doesn't *run* into the classroom, he *explodes* into it. Roger doesn't just pack a suitcase with toys; instead, he stuffs his green duffel bag with very specific images. They may comment on the effectiveness of the title, the believability of the things that happen, and anything else.

Conclude the discussion of this essay by asking your students one final question: "Other than the author, who else could have written this exact story?" The answer will likely be "no one," since it is the story of how one person—Roger—affected the life of the author.

That's when you tell your students their assignment: to write about someone in their lives who, like Roger, appeared for only a short time but who left a huge impact.

Note: You may use one of the student samples that was published in *Creative Kids* instead of "Roger and Jim" for this introductory discussion, or you may go over two or all three of the essays if it seems appropriate. It may be inspiring for students to see student work that has been published.

To further inspire your students, consider showing the "Yes, Middle Schoolers *Can* Write This Well" sheet of one-liners written by eighth-grade students. Show one sentence at a time, and ask students to infer the fuller context of the essays from which the lines came. The main point in sharing these excerpts is to show students how much meaning—and emotional power—can be found in even a very brief writing passage. Help them understand that they, too, are capable of writing power-packed sentences, if they include precise details and real emotional moments.

3. Invite Students to Complete Their Own Responses

If you have time left in the class period, allow students to brainstorm about whom they want to write. They will likely have some questions, such as:

- **"Does it have to be a real person?" "Does it have to be a person *at all?*"** You can decide the answer to these questions, but we have allowed students to write about pretty much anything: pets, dolls, imaginary friends, etc. If you are liberal about what you'll accept as a subject, you are more likely to get strong, heartfelt responses. (In the sample on page 76, "My Gygy," the author wrote about the blanket he loved as a young child, which he said was like a Siamese twin to him.)

- **"When you say the person was in your life for only a short time, does this mean the person died?"** Not necessarily. It might be that a best friend moved away, a parent left home due to divorce, a coach stopped working with a team, or a relationship with someone you cared about ended because you simply grew apart.

- **"What if the person was *always* there, but you didn't realize it?"** This is often a relative with whom the student had little contact early in life, developing a relationship only later. Such a person would be acceptable to choose.

Encourage your students to submit their final drafts to a publication that publishes student work, such as *Creative Kids* and *Teen Ink*. This encouragement to consider sending their work to a "real" audience might prompt some of your writers to put extra effort into their compositions.

> **A Word About Roger**
>
> You may tell any students who ask that after Roger and Jim shared that "one last hug" in Jim's apartment, they never saw each other again. Jim moved to another state at the end of that school year. Although he kept in touch with community members who knew of Roger's living situation, the school district involved would only say that Roger had moved into another foster home in another part of New Hampshire. You may also want to tell your students that this story took place in the 1970s, which may help frame the references in the story.

Finally, remind your students of the most important point of all in completing these essays: no one else in the world will be able to write this story better than they can . . . because they lived it.

Extensions

Classroom Extensions

1. Even though not every essay you receive will be of publishable quality, virtually every one of them will have at least one or two lines that are extremely strong. Compile a list of these powerful sentences, labeling the list, "Yes, Middle Schoolers *Can* Write This Well!" and distribute it to your students. Try this: instead of simply returning the student essays with comments and suggestions, read only one or two sentences from each essay (taken from your compiled list of one-liners) and ask the student who wrote this sentence to come to the front of the class and collect his or her essay. As they collect their essays, consider inviting students to speak for a minute about the subject of the story, providing some context to this one line you just read aloud.

2. After you return the essays to your students, have each one highlight *another* line from their story that they especially like. Then, in random fashion, students select one of their classmates' "one liners" and write an essay, factual or fictitious, using this line as a central theme.

3. Share your own essay with your students, either prior to or at the conclusion of this activity. In fact, one of the better ways to do this is to highlight one line from your own essay and, when no one claims it as theirs, admit that it is your writing. At that point, you may read your essay to the class.

4. Another way of publishing student essays is to post them on your class website or blog. To ensure that your writers get an audience, consider emailing families to encourage them to navigate to the website. You can also use a class or school newsletter or Twitter to ask other teachers and adults to stop by, read a few essays, and leave a comment.

School Extension

If other teachers in your team or grade are willing to do this activity, select all essays that you believe might merit publication and invite these students to a special lunch. At this lunch, encourage these students to consider revising their essays (using your suggestions for doing so) for publication. If students choose to undertake this challenge, allow them to complete the revisions in lieu of another writing assignment that your other students will complete.

Family Extension

Depending on the content of each essay, it may or may not be appropriate to share these stories with the person who is the subject of them. However, for stories that have a positive message or uplifting tone, invite students to send their essays to the people they wrote about, if they have a way of contacting them, accompanied by a letter as to why they chose this individual.

Roger and Jim by Jim Delisle

Roger's entrance explodes the silence of my small, square classroom: fists bloodied, cheeks streaked with tears, his once-white shirt stained and soaked with sweat. He has had another fight.

This time, Roger knows there is no second chance; he must go away once again. As before, his short fuse was ignited by the comments of other kids. And, as before, he now regrets having gone out for recess and exposed himself to these taunts.

He is sobbing and breathing, sobbing and breathing, trying to mouth the words "I'm sorry" through his tense, quivering lips. All that comes out is air. As his teacher, as his father, I hold him close. His blood and sweat now stain my clothes as well.

Roger is 14, but his strong body belies his youth. He struggles to free himself from my tight, containing embrace. I respond by loosening my grasp, but he clings to me all the more. We share closeness, however it was earned.

Roger and I have not always been son and father. Last year, he had another father, and before that still another. Roger is a foster child, a perennial orphan, returning to his biological parents only when we well-intentioned others give up.

When he is with his parents, Roger usually sits glued to the TV, his lips parted by the butt of a cigarette that they first dared him to try. He cannot go to school in his hometown, having been expelled too many times. That's all right with Roger's parents because it gives him more time to chop wood (the family's only source of heat), fetch water (when the pipes freeze, the backyard spring still gurgles), and be a diversion for those two lonely adults who are tired of having only each other for company. It's all right with Roger, too. At least he doesn't get into fights at home, and he can fulfill the assignments of his parents much more easily than he can those of his teachers.

But, the state said "no," and Roger was placed recently in the care of a couple in a nearby town where he could go to school. They had been his foster parents before I came along, and it was a fight—like today's—that transferred him from their home to mine.

In fact, Roger has had many fathers in his 14 years; many mothers, too. His foster brothers and sisters probably remember him more clearly than he remembers them. Words like *sister* and *father* have no permanence for him; they serve only to identify those people with whom he is currently living and eating.

Roger and I walk up the corridor toward the principal's office. We are met by the startled stares from teachers whose heads turn to watch this wounded pair. They wonder—some out loud—why a 23-year-old teacher takes on the responsibilities of a child who is feared and often hated by his peers.

The principal talks. I try to listen, but attend instead to Roger's quiet sobs and sniffles. Looking downward, I see my hands trembling, so I grab one with the other. Roger hears the principal's words, but understands few—he is mentally retarded, the state said so.

No more chances for Roger. Suspension didn't work, neither did the principal's threats after previous fights. I suspect Roger remembers these threats only when he is calm. When he gets angry, he hits.

We leave the office, then the building. I don't look back—I'll be there again tomorrow. But, Roger gives a parting glance to the art display where his papier-mâché skier smiles back at him. It had earned him third prize and a brief moment of positive attention from a surprised student body. Now, it is just a remnant.

continued →

"Roger and Jim" originally appeared in *Barefoot Irreverence: A Collection of Writings on Gifted Children* (2002) by James R. Delisle, pp. 5–7. Prufrock Press.

From *Building Strong Writers in Middle School: Classroom-Ready Activities That Inspire Creativity and Support Core Standards* by Deb Delisle and Jim Delisle, copyright © 2011.

Roger and Jim (continued)

The ride home is quiet. Roger's dried blood flakes on my car's white seats. He pokes the bits of blood, crunching them into still smaller pieces. He looks down at his discolored clothes, plays with the shoelaces of his Keds, and whimpers.

Suddenly, I think that Roger may have been hurt in the fight, that perhaps his tears are caused by a cracked rib or a chipped tooth. I pull the car onto the shoulder of the road. "Nothing hurts," he says. "I'm just sad."

Roger's bedroom is crowded with Kiss posters and homemade cloth-and-paper airplanes. The top of his bureau is cluttered with the latest Matchbox cars. An assortment of his already-worn clothes connects bed and hamper; only a few shirts have made it to the laundry bin. Roger sits, staring outside at the crisp morning with its melting snow—the last time he will see this view.

I call our social worker. Roger overhears and begins to pack his few, small possessions into a musty, olive duffel bag. Wood clanks against metal as Tinkertoys strike cars, trucks, and pennies. Then, he returns to his chair, staring outdoors once again.

We have shared so much, Roger and I. The ocean at Hampton Beach, one of my favorite summertime retreats, became Roger's big, salty pool. His first escalator ride, at the National Air and Space Museum, had been a highlight of our trip to Washington, D.C. Even a traffic jam on the Capital Beltway had been fun.

It seemed easy for Roger to see me as "Mr. Delisle" at school and "Jim" at home or on vacation. He played his roles well, and, except for being unable to con me into believing that he had no homework, he kept my roles as teacher and father distinct.

I found it more difficult, as I tried to combine teacher and father in both settings. Maybe it would have helped if I'd given him a title like "Mister" for school and kept "Roger" for home. Maybe.

The social worker's car pulls into the driveway. I walk to Roger's room, swallowing a large and sour lump in my throat.

"You take care, Roger, okay?"

"Okay."

Steve, the social worker, enters. No one looks at anyone else. His last visit had been to deliver some of Roger's winter clothes, and he was pleased with my report on how well Roger was doing. Now, the scene is awkward. Steve clears his throat. I manage a handshake. Roger's eyes glisten, and a tear or two plops onto the blue kitchen carpet.

He turns to me.

"One last hug."

"Okay."

The car backs out of the driveway and soon disappears down the quiet street. Roger will spend the night with his real parents (it'll be cold; they'll probably need wood).

I climb back up to my second-floor apartment, aware of my failure, aware of my grief. Sorting out what went wrong will have to wait until later. I guess I'll have to clean out Roger's desk at school (he had just begun to feel confident about his reading and math), and his bedroom will probably get used for storage once again.

A tear of my own darkens the kitchen carpet. I am sobbing and breathing, trying to mouth the words "I'm sorry" through tense, quivering lips. All that comes out is air.

"Roger and Jim" originally appeared in *Barefoot Irreverence: A Collection of Writings on Gifted Children* (2002) by James R. Delisle, pp. 5–7. Prufrock Press.

From *Building Strong Writers in Middle School: Classroom-Ready Activities That Inspire Creativity and Support Core Standards* by Deb Delisle and Jim Delisle, copyright © 2011.
Free Spirit Publishing Inc., Minneapolis, MN; 800-735-7323; www.freespirit.com. This page may be reproduced for use within an individual school or district.
For all other uses, contact www.freespirit.com/company/permissions.cfm.

Thankful for a
Thanksgiving Change

Our light, wispy knocks on the hard white door bellow throughout the spacious garage. I focus my sight entirely on the door. I stare so hard that I am surprised the door does not become translucent. The cold winter air sends a shiver down my spine and throughout my soul.

"Remember, Uncle Joe isn't doing well. He is especially having trouble breathing. Just be nice and friendly. Don't act like anything has changed," my dad explains to me.

I nod, acting like I understand. I can tell that this is hardest for my dad. He is losing his older brother to an unseen enemy—cancer. The door opening interrupts my thoughts.

"Oh, hey guys," my Aunt Jackie says. "Come on in. Don't worry about taking your shoes off."

We embrace each other and tell one another "Happy Thanksgiving." Walking out of the kitchen and into the dining room, my line of sight focuses on two men sitting at the table. Both have gray and white hair, and it is easy to tell that they are brothers. One jumps up, energy an essence of his very being.

"Hey, everybody!" Mr. Energy gushes. "Happy Thanksgiving! How are you doing?"

We politely reply, hugs and handshakes circling around me. Soon after, the other man greets us. He seems to be the exact opposite, his voice frail and strained. I recall my dad's words: "He is especially having trouble breathing."

I take in a shallow but enormous breath. I look my uncle over once again. He is skinny and small, with thin, short hair. Covering his upper body is a button-down pink shirt. His face looks tired and strained. He looks so frail that I am afraid if he bends he will snap in half. I say, "Hi," but my voice, too, is weak. I wish I could do something about losing my Uncle Joe.

My siblings and I make our way out of the dining room and into the living room. I begin to try digesting what I just experienced, and I am extremely worried. My uncle and I were never extremely close, but I have never seen him in such bad condition. Before, I never felt uncomfortable in his presence. Now, I fear being with him. It isn't him that I'm afraid of, but myself. I fear that I am not doing enough. I am always afraid to say the wrong thing. As the snow outside falls, so does my heart. I come to the shocking realization that there is nothing I can do. This scares me more than anything.

In the living room, I greet my three cousins, Uncle Joe's sons. Once again, I find myself drifting away and dreaming of happier times. Why did I take the cheerful times for granted? Why didn't I indulge in the carefree atmosphere or watch Uncle Joe more closely, so I would never forget what he looked like before cancer attacked him so recklessly? Our relationship had always been weak, like that of two acquaintances. Not friends, not family. For me, that always seemed right. Now, it seems like it was not enough.

What about Uncle Joe's image scares me so much? Is it his skinny body, so limp that I am sure his ribs protrude from his weak stomach beneath his baggy shirt? The helpless look in his eyes? Is he asking for help, or is it merely a meaningless glance? Is the scariest part of his image that it isn't what it used to be?

Perhaps this makes the most sense. Reality is now miles away, and it seems unforgiving and cold. I don't want to come back. I want to stay frozen in the past forever. I finally force myself to come back into the harsh present, into my Aunt Jackie's house. However, most shockingly, I come back to the truth. My Uncle Joe will never be the same.

Eventually, my sister and I leave the room in search for another TV. We find one in my Grandma's old bedroom, and I plop down on the first chair in sight. We half-watch reruns of "Everybody Loves Raymond." The whole time I am pondering what is happening in this house, both to my Uncle and to me.

Uncle Joe briefly enters the room and I am dumbstruck again. I am sure now that the drastic change in image scares me the most. I hold my breath, and he does not say anything. I find that, once again, I cannot find the words to say.

As we leave the house, on that lamentable Thanksgiving, I come to a conclusion: My relationship with my uncle has changed, but we both have one thing that will always stay the same. Love is an unbreakable bond.

Courtney Kral, 15 • • • • •
Twinsburg, OH

"Thankful for a Thanksgiving Change" originally appeared in *Creative Kids*, volume 26, issue #1, Fall 2007, page 26. It is reprinted with permission of Prufrock Press Inc. (www.prufrock.com).

My Gygy

I first received my gygy when I was about 2 years old. Well, I didn't actually receive it; I stole it from my older sister (she was about 4).

At first, it was an off-white blanket with rainbow colored strips. But, as I used it, chewed it, and tore it apart, it became a stringy rag that smelled and always fell apart.

Very rarely did you see me without my gygy or my gygy without me—it was almost like we were connected. If I had to go to the store with my mom or dad, it was there, and when I ate dinner, it was there. It was there when I was scared or when I needed a hug or when no one else was around. And, of course, when I slept, it was there. It was even there when I bathed; that was the only time I can remember it getting clean. It became part of me as I became part of it. It was like a Siamese twin to me, my first brother.

But, as I said, it was only a blanket at first. I used to tear it apart to the point where it no longer took the shape of a blanket, but as my gygy, and that's what it was. I can still remember the stench it brought to my nose as I smelled it and the taste it brought to my mouth as I devoured it apart. Now, those senses would be grotesque to me, but when I was 2, they were the scent and taste of warmth and comfort.

I was unable to sleep without it at night. My gygy seemed to make all the monsters go away. It seemed to put the magic sand in my eyes. It was as important to me as my mom tucking me in at night. I had to have it with me or else I was unable to fall asleep.

I can remember that night, that horrible night, as if it were happening as I write this story. I had just finished brushing my teeth and putting on my pajamas. I came out of my bedroom and went into the kitchen for my gygy, for I had left it there after dinner. When I went to look on the seat, I saw only the seat and the seat alone. I thought nothing of it and thought I had left my gygy next to my toothbrush. No, it wasn't there. I checked my room and it wasn't there either.

This couldn't be happening to me. I had never gone a night without the comfort of my gygy. I called

for my mom and asked her if she had seen it anywhere. All she said in reply was "no." I asked everyone in the house, but no one recalled seeing it. My gygy was gone.

Oh, the sadness inside was indescribable—deep and endless. So, I did what any 6-year-old would do in a time like this: I cried. I cried and cried and cried. Everyone tried to comfort me, but there was no comfort like that of my gygy. I can remember my sister holding me and telling me that everything was going to be fine. But, how could things be fine without my gygy? It was lost and so was I. I remember my mom holding me in her arms and kissing me on my forehead. I must have fallen asleep crying, because I don't remember closing my eyes or even laying down. But, I did sleep, even without my gygy.

I came down the hall for breakfast the next day, just like every morning. And, my whole day was the same as every other day, except my gygy wasn't there. But, to tell you the truth, I felt the same as when my gygy *was* there.

Later in the day, my mom came to me with her hands behind her back. She told me to pick a hand and then she pulled out my gygy. She had found it and washed it for me. As I looked at it, for the first time in my life I saw what it really was, a smelly rag that was falling apart. And, from that moment on, it never meant the same to me again.

It still is with me, but it isn't a part of me like it was. It hangs in my closet every day, not as something to hold when I'm scared, but as a remnant of something that used to be of great importance to me. It hangs there not as a blanket or stringy rag, but as something that used to be my other half, my old Siamese twin, my brother, my gygy.

Joseph Sicurezza, 15 • • • •
Reminderville, OH

"My Gygy" originally appeared in *Creative Kids,* volume 26, issue #1, Fall 2007, page 14. It is reprinted with permission of Prufrock Press Inc. (www.prufrock.com).

Yes, Middle Schoolers *Can* Write This Well!

- She helped me in more ways than anyone else ever has. If I wrote them all down, it would take up a million pages. One page for each day she spent with me.

- The turn, the evil turn I had been anticipating, had arrived.

- It was not the award that made a difference. It was the teacher who gave it to me.

- We didn't sit down and talk. She didn't tell me stories. She taught me things by *not* being there.

- Honestly, what joy can dogs get from sticking their heads out of moving cars?

- Walking into the funeral home out of the rain that seemed to permeate my soul, I realized I had never really known him—my own grandfather.

- The few memories I have of him are locked away in unknown parts of my mind or videotapes from my younger years.

- He stares at the walls like he is in a deep conversation with them. This is what he taught me: too much of something you love can be bad.

- I always kept this pain in my heart because I knew what I was doing was wrong. My parents raised someone better than this.

- I wish my mom would have taken a lot more photos.

- The snow was falling in blankets, as if to tuck the sidewalk in, like a mother does her child every night before he drifts to sleep.

- I walked down the matted carpet, with footprints of people who have come and gone, each one with a story, each one with a past. And now, my brother was to be added to this bunch.

- You know what? I can't remember if I knelt and paid respects. I did at home.

- My dog Scarlett is just like my great-grandmother: she's old, short, and stubborn.

- There was me, in my overalls with cake all over my chubby, smiling face, and him, with his cinnamon-brown hair and that killer smile.

- I love my dad and I wish I never had to leave him. It's not the kid's job.

- I never told anyone the following story, except God in my good-night prayers.

- I will never return to my old, gray, lethargic lifestyle because I have gained so much by living a life filled with color.

- There are so many ways my brother is cooler than I am. I couldn't possibly list them all without my dad getting mad for using up all the ink cartridges.

- I will always be comforted, even in the mortal darkness creeping in upon me as an old woman, by the memories and all we have achieved and done in our younger years, when the most important lessons are learned. And I will be able to smile.

12. The ABCs of Journaling

Young adolescents have many stories to tell and secrets to keep. Sometimes, they will share their experiences and anxieties with anyone who is willing to listen; other times, though, their greatest confidant is the privacy of their own journal. There, they reveal good news and bad, breakups and make-ups, and questions about their yesterdays, todays, and tomorrows. The honest aches and joys of growing up can be the stuff of future novels, short stories, or screenplays. Every writer begins somewhere, so why not encourage our students as soon as we can?

This activity is both public and private. Students begin by sharing their thoughts about particular questions with a small group of classmates. Then they retreat individually to a quiet place where personal writing can begin. The end results, as you shall see, reinforce our belief that adolescents in search of understanding themselves and the world around them have an instinctive wisdom that is open to all who are willing to listen to them.

Product	A 26-sentence essay that reveals the student's thoughts about an issue that is personal, philosophical, or both; each sentence in the essay begins with a different letter, beginning with the letter of the student's choice, with each subsequent letter used in alphabetical order
Materials	• 1 copy of the lesson plan "Journaling, Journeying: Waterfalls of Words and Wonder" (page 81) for each student • 2 "fun" containers (for example a goldfish bowl and a hat) • 1 display copy of the sample student essay, "How Have I Changed Since Last Year at This Time?" (page 82) • 2 copies of the "Questions for Student Responses" handout (page 83) cut into single question strips and inserted, one copy each, into the two containers (you may add questions of your own on the blank lines) • 5–10 ABC picture books (even if they are designed for beginning readers) • 1 or 2 more complex ABC books, such as *The Weighty Word Book* by Paul M. Levitt, Douglas A. Burger, and Elissa S. Guralnick • 1 or 2 thesauruses (or access to an online thesaurus such as www.merriam-webster.com)
Time	Two 45-minute class periods: one to introduce and begin the activity, followed by a homework assignment to complete the essay, and the second for students to share their work with one another
Common Core State Standards	Activity meets standards 1–4, 6–8, 12–16, 18, and 19 from the chart on page 5.

Activity Steps

1. The Hook

Without any explanation, begin reading aloud one of the ABC books as if your students were first graders—circulate around the room, showing individual students the pictures in the book and asking simple questions like "Do you see the aardvark?" or "Can anyone spot the leopard?" Do this with a second ABC book, or, alternatively, ask one of your students to read the book to the class with the same inflection and enthusiasm that you just did. No doubt, this will result in some snickers and confusion; don't be surprised if you hear, "Why are you reading an alphabet book to us? We already know how to read!"

There . . . you've hooked them!

2. Introduce the Activity

Tell your students that the reason you began with such simple books is that most of them probably enjoyed alphabet books when they were just learning to read. Ask if any of them remembers any specific ABC books from their childhood and, if so, why they liked them. At this point, share some alphabet books that are quite complex (we enjoy *The Weighty Word Book,* but your media specialist will likely have other examples, too), to show students that not all alphabet books are intended just for little kids.

Next, begin reading the essay "How Have I Changed Since Last Year at This Time?" asking if the students can pick out the "gimmick" the author used in composing this essay. (The gimmick is that in this 26-sentence essay, every sentence begins with a different letter of the alphabet. If you display the essay, students may more readily find the gimmick than if they just hear it.)

Once students have figured out the gimmick, ask them to listen to the response once again, focusing on both the content (the author's main ideas) and the sentence structure (many sentences begin with clauses or other writing techniques that make reading more interesting). End by asking, "Can anyone guess what your assignment is going to be?"

3. Invite Students to Complete Their Own Responses

Distribute the "Journaling, Journeying" handout, which gives students instructions for how to structure their essays. Then, one by one, have students select two paper strips from either of the two containers, take the selected papers back to their desks, and read over the questions.

Once everyone is seated with two questions, allow *one full minute* for students to think about possible responses to both questions. No writing during this time. After a minute, allow two to three minutes for students to write down some ideas for possible responses to the questions.

Next, have students gather in groups of two or three and spend ten minutes sharing their questions and getting ideas from others about how to respond to them. When they're done chatting, go over the assignment's parameters:

- A 26-sentence essay that responds to a question the student drew

- Each sentence in the essay begins with a different alphabet letter

- Whatever letter begins the essay, the next sentence begins with the next letter alphabetically, and the next sentence begins with the next letter, following the alphabet sequentially until all 26 letters are used. (So, if the essay's first sentence begins with "S," the next sentence begins with "T," then "U," and so on. This essay would end with a sentence beginning with the letter "R.")

Finally, disperse students to "quiet areas" within the classroom, in the hall, or at the library to begin writing.

Remind students that they are writing an essay that should make logical sense from beginning to end—they are not writing random sentences! Review the "Some Extra Stuff" section of the "Journaling, Journeying" handout, which allows students, among other things, to substitute the prefixes "Ex-" or "Ox-" for the letter "X."

If students are absolutely stumped by the questions they selected initially, you may allow them to choose two new ones.

End the class period by asking if the students have additional questions about the assignment. If not, provide a timeline for completing the assignment at home (we'd suggest no more than two nights), using whatever parameters you wish (for example, responses must be typed, first words of each sentence in bold or italic print, etc.)

Extensions

Classroom Extensions

1. Even though it may sound like a good idea for every student to read his or her essay aloud to the class, we have found that many students stop listening after the first few essays. Instead, we suggest that students get back in their original small groups to share. Each group should be given the option of "electing" an essay that they believe everyone should hear. You may wish to have the students turn in their essays for you to read before students share them in small groups, as you may find an outstanding example for the other students to hear.

2. If time allows and student interest is strong, ask students to add an illustration to their responses. These, along with the essays, could be displayed in a prominent place outside the classroom.

3. In addition to the 32 example questions enclosed here, include two strips in each container that read "Write your own question . . . and answer it."

4. If any of your students speak another language fluently, you may have them compose the response to their question using that language and its alphabet.

5. For students who have responded to the same question, have them compare and contrast their responses.

6. If any of your students already keep a diary or journal, invite them to add this response to it. If not, invite your students to make this response the first entry in a new diary or journal.

School Extensions

1. If your school has a broad range of grade levels, have your older students ask these same questions to younger students, recording the younger kids' responses. Then, the two students can work together to write the essay in the sequential alphabet format, using some or all of the alphabet.

2. Ask your teaching colleagues to answer a common question—for example, "What are the most rewarding aspects of teaching?"—in the same format as students have answered their questions. Then, highlight one essay a week by placing it in a prominent location (for example, the cafeteria) where students can read it.

3. Hold an "Alphabet Book Rally" at which students select their favorite ABC books and read them to small groups of younger children at one of your district's primary schools.

Family Extension

Have students choose a question and ask various family members to complete the same assignment, but with this variation: Divide the alphabet into sections, so each family member does part. For example, Dad writes by using the letters A–F for his response, Mom uses the letters G–L to answer this same question, and so on. If younger family members are used, the question could be an "easier" one, like "What is the most fun part of growing up?" or "What animal would make the world's perfect pet?"

Journaling, Journeying: Waterfalls of Words and Wonder

Imagine telling (or writing) a story that lets your readers know both who you are and what you believe. It's as simple as *A . . . B . . . C.*

Here's your assignment: Write a 26-sentence essay that responds to one of the questions you picked, in which each sentence begins with a different letter of the alphabet. Choose a letter to begin with, then begin each subsequent sentence with the next letter in the alphabet. For example, if your first sentence begins with "C," your next sentence must begin with "D," the next sentence with "E," and so on. The last sentence in your essay would begin with "B."

These rules will make the writing trickier than normal, but don't focus only on the alphabetical ordering. You are not only writing *sentences*, you are composing a *response to the question you selected*. Your essay needs to make sense.

Some Extra Stuff

1. Not all of your sentences need to be complete sentences—some can be phrases or even single words. Don't overdo this technique, but it can be used effectively for several alphabet letters.

2. For the letter "X," you may use words that have "X" as the second letter (like "example," "axe," or "oxymoron").

3. If you get stuck for good opening words, use a thesaurus for reference.

4. Your work will be displayed for others to see and read, so please do not use names that are real—unless, of course, you are complimenting or thanking that person.

The ABCs of Journaling
Sample Student Essay, *Serena, 8th grade*

How Have I Changed Since Last Year at This Time?

Life is precious. Many things happen for a reason, even though we may not always know what the reason is. Not once will I waste my time doing something stupid, because this year I have changed how I live each day of my life. Often, I think about all of the people I've known who have passed away, and if they lived their lives the best they could each day. Probably not. Quietly, I think to myself every day, "have I lived this day so that if I would die this very minute, I would be satisfied with how I lived it?" Respecting the small things in life has helped me be more thankful than I have ever been before.

Sadly, this summer I was faced with a lot of deaths and a lot of people getting sick and injured. This made me think about some things. Usually, I would just think about the family that it happened to. Various times, now, I think about my family and myself. What would happen if something like that happened to me or someone in my family? Exactly the reason why I think so much about this each day. You never actually realize it could happen to you . . . until it does. Zestful days go by where things go perfectly, and others go by when you just want to have nothing to do with them.

Accept what you have and be thankful for it. Because you never know what the rising sun will bring. Care for your family and friends. Deal with issues you go through each day and try to make them better. Especially, when other people need you. Follow your dreams. Go for your goals. Hold on to the special things you have in life. Increase the happy times in your life so that you can also make the people around you happy. Just remember to live every day to the limit, as I now try to do. Keep these things in mind each day you live.

Questions for Student Responses

What do you think your mom or dad was like at your age?

What is it that makes you unique among everyone else?

What do we owe to other people?

Describe an act for which you would like to be remembered.

Can a person work *too* hard at something?

How have you changed since last year at this time?

Why do people in groups sometimes do things they would not normally do on their own?

What one thing have you always wanted to tell someone you know?

Explain how a single leaf falling from a tree to the ground can have an effect on the world.

What is the greatest lesson you ever learned?

How do you know you are awake and not just dreaming?

What question (besides this one) really bothers you?

Can telling the truth ever be wrong?

Describe your favorite elderly person.

How do you "get away" on your own when you can't go anywhere?

How are you *not* the way you seem to others?

What is the weirdest thing that ever happened to you?

If you could live anywhere else, where would it be? Why?

What is one of the most memorable things someone has ever done for you?

Do people have a responsibility to take care of one another?

What are the qualities of the best teachers?

Describe the greatest gift you ever gave to someone.

Are all people created equal?

What is the most important lesson you have ever learned from a fictional character?

Explain the meaning of "innocence."

Describe a "masterpiece" you will create someday.

Why do good people sometimes have to suffer?

When should people control, and *not* control, their emotions?

Who among your friends or family understands you the best?

Is it ever okay to break a promise?

Can someone who is not very intelligent teach other people anything?

_____

_____

Whose hero are you?

_____

_____

Writing to Make a Difference

Good writing matters. When a sentence or paragraph can bring a tear to your eye or a smile to your face, the writer has succeeded because he or she has changed the way you see the world. Whether they're in a novel, speech, poem, or song, words can make you see things from a new perspective. Take these sentences from the best-selling coming-of-age novel, *The Highest Tide*, by Jim Lynch:

- "She babysat me so much in the early years she smelled like family."

- "In the span of a week I'd gone from feeling proud when I made her lunch to feeling guilty when I didn't."

- "It takes time to trust the earth again once you've seen it move. It even looks different, the way your father looks different after he spanks you."

- "I marched her apology back through my head so many times I couldn't remember the differences between what she'd said and what I'd hoped to hear."

Even taken out of context, these sentences from Miles, the 13-year-old "pink-skinned, four-foot-eight, seventy-eight-pound soprano" protagonist of *The Highest Tide* speak eloquently to the power of well-crafted words: their ability to draw readers into a world inhabited by people you've never met, but whom you feel you have always known.

Young adolescents are living, breathing dichotomies: they crave independence while savoring the comfort of established routines; they seek to stand out from the crowd while remaining one of the gang; and they want to make a difference in a world they may not have experienced much. The writing activities in this section are designed to help students see the many ways in which their lives intersect with others—and to help them see how their words can affect the lives of others.

Learning Objectives

- To give students the opportunity to see how their personal writing can have a positive impact on the lives of others

- To provide writing lessons that capitalize on the growing maturity of students by asking them to reflect upon significant events in their own lives

- To expand student vocabulary by asking them to create writing samples that use precise, "visible" nouns and verbs to create a sense of mood

13. Help, Hope, Hurray!

Some of the best resource materials we have used with our students did not come from textbooks but were delivered in the daily mail or newspaper. For example, one of our young friends, Jason Crowe, was highlighted in a two-page article in *People* magazine when he was 13 years old for his efforts on behalf of the American Cancer Society (ACS).

Jason's grandmother, "Nanny," had died of pancreatic cancer when Jason was nine years old, devastating him to the point where his parents were concerned about his well-being. They decided they needed to help him cope with his grandmother's death in a way that was constructive, not destructive, to his young life. Because Nanny was the person who taught Jason to read and write when he was three years old, his family decided to help Jason honor his grandmother by helping others using the language tools with which she had equipped him. Thus was born *The Informer*, a small-town newspaper whose subscription sales would go to the ACS, in the hope of eradicating the disease that had taken Jason's Nanny from him.

What began as a small-scale project quickly escalated into a global phenomenon, as word of mouth (and the article in *People)* helped grow Jason's paper into a publication distributed in 30 U.S. states and more than two dozen nations. Its main contributors were other children around the globe who believed their life stories and accomplishments could inspire others to social action. Ten years later when Jason headed to college, *The Informer* published its last edition. *The Informer* had raised several thousands of dollars for the ACS and other nonprofit organizations. We can only imagine how proud Nanny must be of her grandson!

Jason Crowe is not alone in being able to make a positive difference in the world. In this activity, your students will be able to begin their own journey into societal change.

Product	Many and varied, including but not limited to: letters to the editor of a local newspaper or website; personal letters to individuals who need help or a "thank you" for their contributions to a better world; and schoolwide public service projects conceived and directed by students
Materials	• Various media accounts of individuals or companies working to improve the lives of others: consider copies of local newspapers (in print or online); magazines such as *People* that feature such stories; books such as *Real Kids, Real Stories, Real Change* by Garth Sundem; and websites such as www.myhero.com and www.unicef.org (click on "Unicef People" then "Young Leaders") • 1 copy of "Help, Hope, Hurray!" handout (page 90) for every four to six students • 1 display copy of the sample "Help, Hope, Hurray!" student activities (page 91) • 1 display copy of Ebony and Miracle's letter to Nick (page 92)
Time	One 45-minute class period to introduce the activity and get students started researching, choosing a topic, and choosing a response; assign the completion of the project as homework
Common Core State Standards	Activity meets standards 2, 3, 4, 6, 12, 14, 15, and 16 from the chart on page 5.

Activity Steps

1. The Hook

Prior to introducing this activity to your students, use the sources suggested in the materials section and others to gather a collection of five to ten examples of people who have gone the extra mile on behalf of others. The stories do not have to be earth-shattering in their impact; rather, they might be as simple as an individual who has collected books for children living in homeless shelters, a teenager who began a canned food drive for her community, or a grandmother who takes the bus each week to read to children in a nearby hospital.

When your students arrive, place them in groups of four to six, distributing one of the collected stories to each group. Ask one student per group to read the story aloud to the other group members. Once students have read their selections, ask a member from each group to summarize the story's content to the rest of the class.

When this is completed, ask the class what the different stories have in common, and write their responses on the board. Next, ask for volunteers to provide examples of others they know or have heard about who have done similar projects on behalf of others. End this discussion by stating something like this: "These individuals need to be thanked or encouraged or helped, don't you think?"

2. Introduce the Activity

Distribute the blank "Help, Hope, Hurray!" handout (one per group) and go over the three types of responses together:

- A "help" response is the most complex and involved. The student writes to the person or organization to offer assistance in getting past a challenge. This might be direct assistance, such as offering to organize or participate in a fundraiser, or it could be indirect, such as spreading the word about a worthy organization or event by writing a letter to the editor. Encourage students to use their imaginations when thinking of how they could offer help, but stress that if they *offer* help, they need to be prepared to follow through.

- A "hope" response involves encouraging a person or an organization that is currently facing a challenge or doing something good for others. It can be a letter, an email, or a creative note (like an art project) that says, essentially, "You can do it!"

- A "hurray!" response is for people or organizations who have accomplished something commendable. This is a thank you or congratulations that can come in the form of a personal missive, an art project (involving writing, of course), a letter to the editor, or another public display that recognizes the do-gooders for the work they've done.

The differences between these three types of responses may sometimes be vague, and sometimes a response may involve more than one type. A "help" response, for example, will almost certainly offer "hope" as well, and a "hurray!" or a "hope" may feel like "help" to a recipient. Students should understand these types of responses, and for this group work they will be asked to categorize the stories they find into the types of responses that seem most appropriate. But when students work on their actual responses, encourage them not to get bogged down in what type, exactly, they are doing. In the end, what's important is that the response supports someone who needs or deserves it, and that the students see their writing go out to a real audience and have a real effect.

After you've discussed the "Help, Hope, Hurray!" handout, pass out the media resources described in the materials section so every group has several sources. If you have access to the

Internet in your classroom, you can direct students to the websites listed and even allow them to conduct general Internet searches. Direct the groups to look for stories about people or groups who are going through a challenge or doing good for others—people they believe qualify for a help, hope, or hurray.

As students look for stories about individuals and/or organizations, ask them to think about what they might say to the people if they were to meet them. After a few minutes, ask a representative from each group to tell the class about one or two stories their group selected and explain a response they might give to the people involved.

3. Invite Students to Complete Their Own Responses

Now it's time for students to work alone (or you can allow them to pair up if you like) on finding their own stories and crafting their own responses. They can use one of the stories their group identified, or they can find a new story. Allow the rest of the class period for students to identify their stories and, if time permits, begin their responses. Provide a deadline that is two to three days out for responses to be turned in to you. A second copy should be sent out—to the person or organization in the story; to the newspaper, magazine, or website where they hope to have a letter to the editor published; or to whatever recipient they may be addressing.

Note: Every student's response must have an audience outside the classroom. A large part of the value of this activity is exposing student writing to a larger, real-world audience.

Most of your students will likely want to contact the person or organization directly with a letter or email of appreciation or thanks. You can expand their repertoire of possible responses, though, by showing them the "Help, Hope, Hurray!" student samples, which show other ways students have responded to this assignment. Do not downplay the effect of contacting someone by letter or email (you might also share the letter written by Ebony and Miracle to show how effective such responses can be), but let your students get creative with the format their responses could take.

If you so desire, tell your students that the activity you begin today is one that may resurface throughout the year, depending on their level of interest and the number of people they find through their reading who need help, hope, or hurray.

Extensions

Classroom Extensions

1. Not every student in your class will feel the drive to extend helping hands to others. However, for those who do, you might gather together a committee of students called your Person-to-Person Committee. These volunteers will scan newspapers and magazines on a regular basis, and suggest to you and other class members people who need one of the "3 Hs." Committee members can either assign themselves the task of being your classroom ambassadors in responding, or they can seek additional volunteers within the classroom or school.

2. If any of the persons who received one of the "3 Hs" from your class writes back or contacts you in any other way, you might consider inviting that person to speak to your students. This is a great way to instill in students the merits of their efforts. If you have a Person-to-Person Committee (see extension #1), it can lead the way in orchestrating these visits.

School Extension

If your school has a Leadership Team or Student Council, this activity can be a great way to include the entire school in reaching out to the local or world community. A side benefit, of course, is that such a widespread collection of kids working on behalf of others also means that more children than ever will be reading newspapers and magazines to find people who could benefit from one or more of the "3 Hs."

Family Extension

Some terrific ideas for people to contact can come from parents' suggestions, so invite family members to nominate individuals or groups with whom they have contact. Be sure to get back to the parents if your students choose to follow through with their suggestions, or if not, simply thank them for sending in a nominee's name.

One word of caution: Students may need to be reminded to be sensitive about their word choices if they elect to write letters, especially to people who are suffering. For example, in one of our projects, seventh graders wrote to Dr. Richard Olney, a researcher of ALS (Lou Gehrig's disease) who was stricken by the disease he was trying to cure. ALS is always fatal, so it would have been inappropriate for students to write, "I know you will get better." Once our students understood the sensitivity of their words, they made sure their letters included other sentiments, including thanks for the work Dr. Olney had done and admiration for his continued work with ALS patients. Consider reading all letters before they are sent to make sure they are appropriate.

As an aside, Dr. Olney responded to the students who wrote to him, thanking them for their "recent, extraordinary letters. I am deeply touched that you chose to make such an effort on my behalf. I am amazed that words from so far away can feel so close."

Help, Hope, Hurray!

Search through newspapers, magazines, or other sources to find one or more stories about people who could use **Help, Hope,** or a **Hurray!** Write enough information about the person and situation to explain it to others. Also, write down the source (publication, page number, and date) where you found the story.

Help

Assistance for people or organizations going through a challenging time.

_____

_____

_____

_____

_____

_____

_____

_____

Hope

Encouragement for people facing a challenge or seeking a goal that may be difficult to reach.

_____

_____

_____

_____

_____

_____

_____

_____

Hurray!

Acknowledgment or thanks for people who are working to make life better for others or who have overcome a difficult challenge.

_____

_____

_____

_____

_____

_____

_____

_____

Help, Hope, Hurray!
Student Samples

Hurray! After reading about Dr. Richard Olney, a San Francisco–based researcher of ALS (Lou Gehrig's disease) who had recently been diagnosed with that disease himself, a group of seventh graders wrote to him letters of encouragement and thanks for his 25 years of involvement with patients who had the disease.

Hope When a school district began a "Stop Smoking" program for its employees, a class of sixth graders designed notes of encouragement in the shape of cigarettes. The notes were written on strips of white paper with the students' names at the ends on brown paper (the cigarette filters) and were placed in a box decorated to look like a pack of cigarettes. Individual "cigarettes" were distributed to the program's participants the first night. Weeks later, a school employee showed up in this class, clutching his "cigarette." "Thanks to you kids," he said, "I've quit smoking."

Hurray! After interviewing World War II veterans in their community for a social studies class, a large group of eighth graders invited the veterans and their families to a special event: a USO (United Service Organizations) show held in the high school auditorium. Students entertained the veterans by playing songs from the 1940s, showing film clips from the era, and doing dance routines that were popular then. Students also read brief essays of appreciation and thanks they had written based on their research and the personal interviews they'd conducted with the veterans. "Bob Hope," a popular entertainer of that era, was the emcee, and the evening ended with a group of eighth graders, in uniform, raising the flag over Iwo Jima as "The Star-Spangled Banner" was played by the high school band.

Help After a family of six lost both parents in fatal accidents within a year, a middle school team decided to help the four children, ages 7–20, by holding bake sales and raffles and sponsoring a school dance to raise money for the family. Within one month, more than $1,200 was collected and presented to the 20-year-old son of the family at a schoolwide assembly.

Hope A class of seventh graders was visited by Nick, a college student with Asperger's syndrome, who spoke of his struggles and successes and answered questions about living with his disorder. Afterward, each student sent Nick a note of thanks and encouragement.

Hope and Hurray! So that soldiers in Iraq would have a feel for home, two classes of U.S. sixth graders designed and created banners and quilts that contained notes of thanks and "Scenes of America" that could be hung in soldiers' barracks. The banners were collected by an Army officer who delivered them to Iraq and emailed the students photos of the banners hanging in various buildings occupied by U.S. soldiers who had received them.

Help, Hope, Hurray!
Example of a Student Letter of Thanks

Dear Nick:

We'd like to thank you very much for speaking to our class last Wednesday. For that 30-minute period, you brought us into your life and taught us about Asperger's syndrome in a way no textbook or teacher could ever do. You brought upon us a new wave of understanding, and we thank you.

The part of your story that probably affected us the most was how you didn't find out you had Asperger's until high school. We know that personally we would be absolutely terrified to find something like that out, especially when we had just started to think we had everything in our lives figured out. It would truly turn our worlds upside-down—how we think and feel—and frankly, we're not sure we would've been able to handle it like you have.

You talked to us with such sincerity and fearlessness that it was inspirational. We will remember your visit—and its message—for a long time. We wish you the best of luck as you continue to study in college to become a special education teacher.

Thank you!
Ebony and Miracle

14. The Cookbook of Life

Well-crafted recipes can lead to brand new experiences. By following step-by-step directions, you let the experience of others lead you toward success. Another great thing about recipes is that you can tweak the ingredients for a little added zest. That added touch of real vanilla instead of its imitation counterpart might make all the difference between a good pie and a great one.

That's part of what makes recipes so appealing. You get the benefit of someone else's expertise, but you have the flexibility to make it your own. In this activity, students draw from their own experience to make recipes that help build a world that's even better, kinder, or more beautiful than it is today.

Product	Each student creates a recipe that shows how to celebrate or improve aspects of our world, and the recipes are compiled into a cookbook suitable for display and sharing
Materials	• Peanut butter and jelly sandwich ingredients (bread, a jar of jelly, and a jar of peanut butter) and a roll of paper towels (be sure you have no peanut allergies in your classroom; substitute with soy nut spread or sunflower seed spread if necessary) • 1 display copy of a list of common measurement terms used in cooking (you can find a list on the Internet at the USDA website or at commercial sites such as www.goodcooking.com) • 1 copy of "The Cookbook of Life" handout (page 96) for each student
Time	Two class periods: one to introduce the activity and brainstorm possible recipes for the book, and another to write and illustrate the recipes; after collecting the recipes, you will need to bind them into a book; the cookbook's debut can occur after the book is bound
Common Core State Standards	Activity meets standards 2, 3, 4, 6, 12, 14, 15, and 16 from the chart on page 5.

Activity Steps

1. The Hook

This is an old routine, but it serves as a fine introduction to hook your students into the need to follow directions if they are going to get the results they desire. Put your students in pairs or groups of three and ask them to write down the step-by-step instructions for making a peanut butter and jelly sandwich. Ask them to be quite precise in their written instructions. Allow about ten minutes for this recipe to be written. As they write, get your peanut butter and jelly ingredients ready.

Collect the recipes from each group, select one of them at random, and ask for a member of the group who wrote it to come up and read it to you. As this student reads, follow the instructions *exactly*. What happens next is both messy and instructive. No doubt, the recipes will make assumptions that are not written down—for example, the recipe may have forgotten to tell you to open the package of bread, so when told to "spread peanut butter on the bread," you spread it on the package. Or if they wrote, "Take a piece of bread in your hand. Put peanut butter on it." Well, . . . does "it" refer to the bread or the hand? You decide . . . and follow the directions literally and precisely. Make two or three sandwiches using the exact directions from your students. No doubt, the gooey concoctions will not resemble the PB&Js that they are used to enjoying.

End this introduction by stating: "There is a reason we have to be precise in giving directions."

2. Introduce the Activity

After cleaning up, or as you clean up, have a class discussion about the students' experiences with recipes. Most likely, some will have quite a bit of experience cooking and following recipes, while others will have none. Ask for examples of easy and difficult recipes, and any stories they have (about themselves or others) of cooking successes and failures. Contribute your own stories, too.

Probe further with the question, "What *other* parts of your life benefit from following precise directions?" Students might say things like "learning to play an instrument," "becoming a good athlete," or "getting good grades at school." Indeed, recipes don't always have to relate to the physical creation of something (like a peanut butter and jelly sandwich); they can also teach you how to improve a life situation like a friendship or a skill like reading or drawing.

Distribute the "Cookbook of Life" handout, and, as you are doing so, ask students if any of them can recall a day when everything went exactly as planned . . . and a day when nothing seemed to go the way they thought it might. After students give several examples, ask them this question: "What if there were 'recipes' we could follow to ensure that things go the way we want them to?"

At this point, tell the students the specifics of this activity: Together as a class, you are going to produce a cookbook whose recipes make not food but tangible and intangible parts of a better world, like "the perfect friend," "the ideal

teacher," "the greenest planet," or "the perfect peace." Students will work in pairs to create at least one recipe per pair.

Go over the handout together and explain the parts of a recipe. Not only will students come up with the ingredients, they will also need to specify the amount of each ingredient that must be used, and, just as with any recipe, the order and manner in which those ingredients need to be combined.

To show the students what you mean by this, ask them to read "A Recipe for a Universe" on the second page of the handout. Afterward, you may want to brainstorm as a class a list of possible topics for recipes, recording these on your board or chart paper for students to consider.

3. Invite Students to Complete Their Own Responses

Ask students to find a partner who wishes to create a recipe for the same topic they do, and have them work in pairs on their recipe. If multiple students want to make recipes on the same topic, we suggest you allow no more than two pairs (two recipes) per topic. If you prefer, you can have students work alone on their recipes so you can see writing from each individual student, but the lively and positive tone of this project does lend itself to a teamwork atmosphere.

Direct students to first compile the ingredients, determine how much of each is needed (display the measurement chart to help provide vocabulary for this), and establish the order (and manner) in which they will be added. They should begin writing the recipe only after they have considered several combinations of ingredients and amounts.

For the final recipes, have students place the ingredients and instructions on the left half of a horizontal 8½" x 11" piece of paper, and have them draw an illustration that covers the right half of the page.

Compiling the books

If you want to keep it simple, bind the pages with staples or a three-ring binder. If you have PowerPoint, it looks nice if you have students make each recipe into a slide that you can then print and laminate (it's simple to paste the text and scan and place photos in Power-Point). Print shops such as FedEx Office can bind the book for a reasonable cost.

Extensions

Classroom Extensions

1. For those students less inclined toward the culinary and more inclined toward cruising the world, have them compile a road atlas instead of a cookbook. The directions are pretty much the same, except the students choosing this option have to determine an end point for a journey (for example, "How to achieve perfect happiness") and the routes they will take along the way. So, will they speed down a super highway or meander down a country road? Will they stop at landmarks along the way (if so, name what they are), or will they just try to reach their destination in record time?

2. Search the Internet for quotes by people who have given their "recipes for success," such as this one by the American scholar William Ward: "Study while others are sleeping; work while others are loafing; prepare while others are playing; and dream while others are wishing." Consider using some of the quotes in a preface for your book.

School Extension

If several grade levels and/or classes do this activity, have a committee of students and teachers select a "best of" recipe collection and compile these into a book that can be sold during your school's book fair, or given as a thank you to visitors who present lessons to students in your school.

Family Extension

Instead of just compiling student-generated recipes, ask students to interview older members of their families (or residents of a nearby nursing home or assisted-living center) with the goal of having them suggest ingredients for a well-lived life. To guide your students in these interviews, you might suggest each student begin by asking, "What are the three most important things that have contributed to your life? What advice would you give to kids my age about what 'ingredients' they need to be happy or successful?" These ingredients can be included as an addendum to the cookbooks the students produce, with the ingredients named most frequently listed first.

Note: If you do this activity in only one classroom, we suggest requiring all your students to do either a recipe or a road atlas so you'll have enough individual pieces to make a book. However, if you do this activity in more than one class, you may allow students to choose and still compile two good-sized books: a cookbook and a road atlas.

The Cookbook of Life

Some days go exactly as planned: you wake up, eat breakfast, go to school, play some video games, do homework, eat dinner, and go to bed. Other times it seems like everything you expect to happen doesn't. Like when the alarm doesn't ring, there's no milk for your cereal, your science teacher is sick and you got the world's meanest substitute, and you miss the bus to go home because you were struggling with your locker combination. Life is like that: sometimes the "ingredients" of our day come together well, and other days our "recipe" for a successful day just doesn't blend smoothly.

But what if you could plan better for the unexpected? What if you could design a surefire way to make life a little more predictable or enjoyable? What if you could create some recipes for success that would work more often than not? That's what this activity is asking you to do: create recipes whose ingredients deal with some of life's big issues.

In this activity, you will contribute to *The Cookbook of Life*, a recipe book like no other. This cookbook does not focus on food, but rather the fundamentals of daily living. For instance, you might want to consider putting together a recipe for:

- a happy family
- the best school
- a well-lived life
- an ideal pet
- a great best friend
- a great vacation
- a memorable teacher
- a greener planet
- a perfect peace

The possibilities are endless.

Of course, your recipes will need some **ingredients.** Consider ideas like humor, patience, kindness, beauty, fun, sunshine, tears, creativity, bravery, tolerance.

You will also need some **measurements** for your ingredients: a cup, teaspoon, smidgen, ton, pinch.

And, of course, you'll need to give some specific **directions:** stir, shake, blend, spice up, bake, freeze, pulverize, boil.

Here is an example:

A Recipe for a Universe

40 cups of stars
1 cup of life
40 tons of planets
39 smidgens of unknown
500 black holes
1 teaspoon of sadness
1 tablespoon of happiness
1 pinch of instinct
1 ton of intelligence
2 bowls of tolerance

Mix the stars, planets, and unknown until they are black with specks of white. While stirring, slowly add black holes. Mix life, happiness, sadness, intelligence, and instinct separately, combining all of these with 1 bowl of tolerance. Pour this mixture into a glass globe and let it chill. Once the universe has gelled, layer in the other bowl of tolerance. Makes one universe.

Note: For parallel universes, double recipe.

—contributed by David, age 12

Once you've gathered your ideas together, write out the recipe on the left side of a horizontal regular size piece of paper, using the other half of the paper to illustrate your recipe.

15. **Placing Thanks**

As teachers, most of us revere holidays. Whether with red hearts on our classroom doors for Valentine's Day or military veterans speaking to our students for Memorial Day or Remembrance Day, educators take the time to acknowledge with their students both the small and big reasons behind our celebrations. Indeed, were it not for holidays, many of us would be at a loss for what to post on our monthly bulletin boards!

One holiday that always seems to entail the same type of assignment, year after year, is Thanksgiving, when students are asked the second-most common question of all classrooms (after "What did you do on your summer vacation?"): "What are you thankful for in your life?"

Responses are written on everything from turkey feathers in elementary schools to extended essays that are shared during announcements in middle schools. These are good assignments, important assignments, because they cause students to reflect on the parts and people in their worlds who helped make them who they are. But . . . the formats for these assignments are often predictable, resulting in boiler-plate answers that, like anything trite, feel shallow over time. And the last thing we want to engender in our students is shallow gratitude.

This assignment—a short one with a lasting impact—requires students to think of thankfulness from a broader perspective. And the format of the project is very appropriate for any celebration that involves food (and which ones do not?): hand-stenciled placemats.

Product	A placemat with the word "Thanks" composed of words and phrases indicating what students appreciate in their lives
Materials	• 1 sheet of white 17" x 22" paper for each student • 1 copy of the "Placing Thanks" handout (page 100) for each student • 1 display copy of the student-completed "Thanks" placemat (page 101) • Thin-lined markers, pens, and colored pencils • Several copies of the "Thanks" template (page 102) for students who want them
Time	One period to introduce and begin the project in class, followed by a homework assignment during which time the final product is completed
Common Core State Standards	Activity meets standards 2, 3, 4, 6, 12, 14, 15, 16, and 18 from the chart on page 5.

Activity Steps

1. The Hook

As students enter the classroom, hand each of them a slip of paper on which you have written something for which you are grateful. Try to make some of the items small and specific, like chocolate ice cream, and some of them larger or less tangible, like Friday afternoons—and everything in between. For example:

- Two-for-one ice-cream sundaes
- The sound of ocean waves
- Photos of my cat
- Cell phones
- The smell of bread baking
- Fire fighters
- Second chances

Don't tell the students what these slips of paper indicate, but ask them to walk around the classroom in silence, sharing their slips with classmates. After a few minutes, invite the students back to their seats and ask them what these items have in common. Then, ask several students to read the item written on their papers. When they do so, respond verbally with why this item is something you cherish, recall fondly, or like a lot. Something like, "I remember when I inadvertently insulted my friend in high school, but he gave me a second chance after I apologized for my mistake." Once you have elaborated on several of these ideas, tell the students that you are going to ask them to reflect on items, people, or ideas that make their own lives more complete.

2. Introduce the Activity

Ask your students if they recall assignments from previous years about being thankful. Most will recall one or more such projects, but don't be surprised if few of the memories are deep or enthusiastic. This may be because the style of the assignment, year after year, looked pretty much the same, or because they were limited to naming one or just a few things they were grateful for, making for predictable responses that varied little from year to year.

Distribute the "Placing Thanks" handout to your students and read through it together. You may want to have a class brainstorming discussion to help the flow of ideas in the various categories: people (both famous and personal), memories, actual items, issues that affect you, and movies or other entertainment. Take a look, too, at the student sample, and consider some of the things Kurt named on his placemat.

Some of the categories, like "issues that are important to me," require serious responses ("too many starving people in the world"), while others like "favorite childhood memories" might tend to be more humorous ("armpit noises in first grade"). Still more are about visible "things in nature" ("a full moon in the summer sky") while others are more ethereal ("an epidemic of peace in the world").

3. Invite Students to Complete Their Own Responses

Have students collate on their handouts at *least* 50 items for which they are thankful, urging them to consider all types of responses, from small to big, from silly to important, and so on, focusing first on the categories listed on the response sheet. Consider putting them in small groups to brainstorm ideas. This will allow them to hear a variety of serious and humorous responses they might not have considered if they had simply started writing down ideas on their own.

Distribute *two* blank sheets of 17" x 22" paper (we all make mistakes!) to your students and have them use the words on their lists to spell out the word "Thanks" (or "Gratitude," should their word list be more extensive) on their sheet of 17" x 22" paper using markers or pens. If students need assistance in making their words resemble the word "Thanks," you may provide the blank template on page 102, and they can simply write their words around the outline. (Be sure to print or copy the template at 200 percent on 17" x 22" paper.) Other students will be comfortable doing their "Thanks" template freehand, as in the student sample.

Assign the finishing of the placemats as homework. You may want to ask them to think of an occasion—a family celebration or national holiday—at which time they could use this placemat and write a brief essay explaining why they chose the occasion. You may even use them during a classroom celebration of writing.

When students turn in their final placemats, laminate them if possible. You may make copies to display in a classroom or hallway collage, returning the original documents to students to use for their intended purpose and person.

Extensions

Classroom Extensions

1. Using the same format as previously described, ask students to create alternative ways to do this assignment. For example, if a classmate is moving to another city, classmates could write their favorite memories into a word that spells out "Good-bye." Or, for a new student, the word "Welcome" could be written out with suggestions students have for making the transition to this new school a successful one. Similarly, for athletes entering into an important game, "Good luck!" can be written out using words of encouragement and support.

2. Combine efforts with the foreign language teacher and have students complete this assignment in the new language they are learning.

3. Although the most typical time to do this activity would be near Thanksgiving, you might also use these placemats for a one-of-a-kind Father's or Mother's Day gift. Or, for an upcoming party, students can complete nameplates, placing each person's individual name on each card, with the words that constitute the letters in the name being that individual's best qualities.

4. Instead of forming the words and phrases students are grateful for into a word, such as "Thanks" or "Gratitude," have them make word clouds (try www.wordle.net). These can be quite beautiful, and they're easily blown up to placemat size.

School Extension

If a teacher is retiring, or a teacher has just had a baby, or a sports team just won a regional tournament, or an academic club just bested a neighboring school . . . on any of these school-wide occasions, make a large banner with words of support, congratulations, or encouragement written on them using this format.

Family Extension

Invite students to ask each member of their families to complete a placemat for another family member after being assigned that person secretly or randomly. These placemats will then be used on the occasion where the entire family gathers.

Placing Thanks

Often, we use national holidays as a time to reflect on the gifts that have been bestowed on us in life. At Thanksgiving, we focus on the bounty that we receive through our families and friends. At New Year's, we look forward to our future while remembering our recent past. On Veteran's Day, we thank those who served to make our country secure and peaceful. These are important days, commemorating important events in our personal or national histories.

But it shouldn't take a special holiday to remind us of the many things for which we are grateful: Small things, like a smile from a friend after a defeat on the field; big things, like the election of someone who you trust and believe in; visible things, like a stunning sunset on a summer evening; and invisible things, like the compassion you feel when you help someone who didn't even ask for your support.

Brainstorm at least five things for which you're grateful in each category below. Consider things big and small for which you are grateful. The more ideas you come up with, the better. When you're done, handwrite these words and phrases into the form of a bigger word, "Thanks" or "Gratitude," to create a suitable-for-use (or framing!) placemat that spells out (literally) those elements of your life that deserve to be acknowledged.

People you know . . . (and like or love)	Famous people you admire
Favorite childhood memories	**Foods and smells**
Objects you love	**Things in nature**
Issues that are important to you	**Music, TV, movies, books**
Intangibles—things you can't see, but you know are there	

MOST VIDEOGAMES. ALBUS DUMBLEDORE.

EXTRA CREDIT PROJECTS. FISHING WITH MY DAD ON A CLEAR LAKE. MTV. CHOCOLATE COVERED PEANUTS.

THE SMELL OF A NEW CAR. SLEEPING LATE ON SATURDAY MORNING. SOLDIERS DEFENDING OUR COUNTRY.

MY YOUNGER BROTHER'S LITTLE LEAGUE GAMES. FACEBOOK. DISNEY WORLD. DIRT BIKES.

MY GRANDFATHER'S WRINKLED FACE. OLD MATCHBOX CARS. AN UNEXPECTED SNOWDAY. MY MOTHER'S LULLABIES.

CANDLES THAT SMELL LIKE CINNAMON. THE STATUE OF LIBERTY. CARAMEL POPCORN.

HOW MY DOG SMELLS WHEN HE'S WET. HALLOWEEN CANDY THAT LASTS FOR A MONTH.

THE BELL THAT SIGNALS THE END OF ANOTHER SCHOOL DAY. TEACHERS (SOME OF THEM...). 3-D MOVIES.

POP ROCKS. A VACATION WHERE PALM TREES GROW. BASKETBALL GAMES WITH MY FRIENDS.

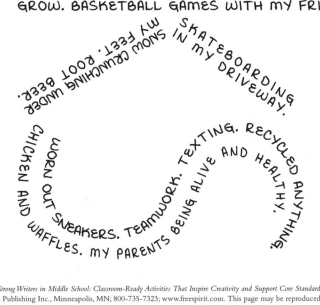

SKATEBOARDING IN MY DRIVEWAY. SNOW CRUNCHING UNDER MY FEET. ROOT BEER. RECYCLED ANYTHING. HEALTHY. TEXTING. TEAMWORK. WORN OUT SNEAKERS. CHICKEN AND WAFFLES. MY PARENTS BEING ALIVE AND HEALTHY.

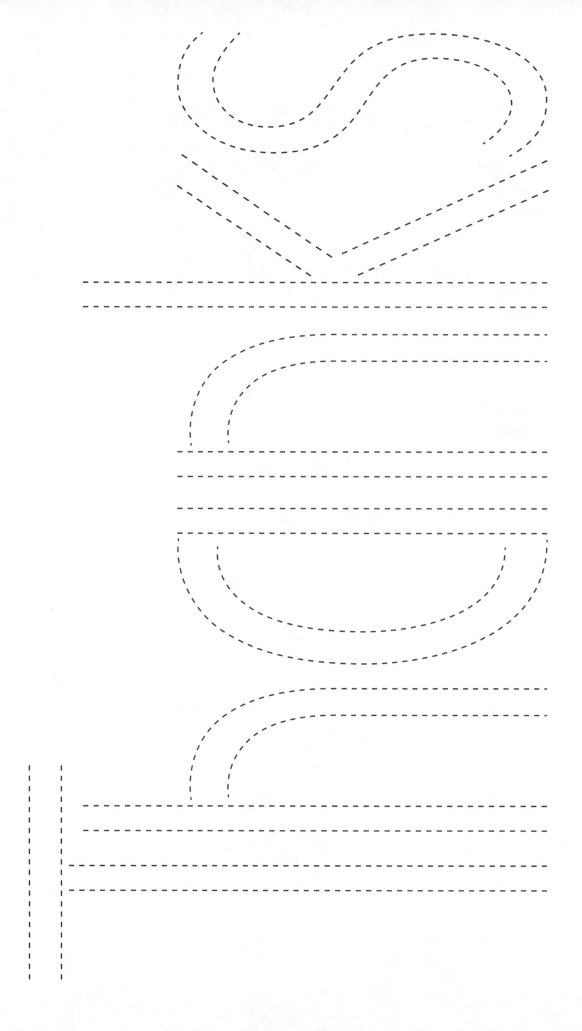

16. W-A-A-A-A-A-Y Beyond Description

Every teacher has one, and this is ours: the favorite activity we do with our students. Over the years, students have responded to "W-A-A-A-A-A-Y Beyond Description" by giving us (and themselves) rich, full responses. Indeed, when students come back to visit from high school or college, the one activity they are apt to recall and talk about is this one.

We learned about this activity while we were working at an independent school in Hong Kong. One evening, one of the guidance counselors (a former teacher of a high school humanities course entailing literature, culture, and religion) leafed through a file drawer and pulled out an example of a lesson he did involving adjectives . . . and much more. Intrigued by his example, we took the lesson back to our students, tweaking it a bit for middle school grades, and tried it out with our sixth through eighth graders. Despite some initial groans about the amount of work and length of time to complete this project, students were virtually unanimous in its worthiness. "I feel like I just finished a writing marathon," said one student, "and I'm exhausted!"

Since then, we've used this activity every year, generally near the end of the year, when students are apt to be the most mature. In sharing this activity with thousands of teachers worldwide, we hear back from many of them with modifications of this lesson's use with younger students, in religious classes, or at adult retreats centered on self-discovery.

Product	A 200- to 400-word essay about a person in the student's life who helped him or her become the person he or she is today; accompanied by a visual symbol (a concrete poem) that is created entirely out of 100 adjectives that the student chooses to describe himself or herself
Materials	• Blank paper and writing implements • Access to thesauruses (hard copies or online versions such as www.merriam-webster.com) • 1 copy of the "W-A-A-A-A-A-Y Beyond Description" instruction sheet (page 106) per student • 1 display copy of the "So Are You . . . " vocabulary quiz (page 107) • 1 display copy of each of the completed student samples (pages 108–111)
Time	Two 45-minute class periods, with additional homework time, to complete the essay and visual; in all, allow one full week for this activity, from the in-class introduction to the presentation of the final products
Common Core State Standards	Activity meets standards 1–4, 6, 12, and 14–19 from the chart on page 5.

Activity Steps

1. The Hook

As students settle at their desks, tell them how excited you are to do this activity with them. Play up how much they are going to enjoy this activity, how students across the globe have found it enjoyable and memorable, etc. Then pull the rug out from under their enthusiasm by telling them that the activity begins with a short vocabulary quiz.

Tell students to pull out a piece of scrap paper (you won't be collecting the quiz results) and display the list of words on the "So Are You . . ." vocabulary quiz. Ask students to select the one word in each pair that describes them better, as each pair of words are antonyms (or have extremely different meanings). Keeping as straight a face as you can, show the first word pair: "ebullient" and "dour." Instruct students to write down which of these two words describes them better. They will protest that they don't know what either of these words means, to which you will respond, "Of course you do. Students of your age know these words."

After displaying the second word pair, "loquacious" and "taciturn," tell your confused students that if they are not sure of either word's meaning, they should simply write the word that *sounds more like them*. After you've done all six word pairs, define each word and have students self-check to determine if they selected words that fit their personalities.

2. Introduce the Activity

As your students complete the quiz, tell them that these complex words may actually appear in their finished assignment. Rather than telling your students what the lesson entails, show them the completed student examples, beginning with the one from Chester.

First, show the 100 adjectives Chester used to describe himself, pointing out three different types of words:

1. "cheap" words, like *cute* and *happy*

2. "expensive" words, like *conscientious* and *unsparing*

3. confusing words, like *old* (how can eighth-grade Chester be old?) and *pacific* (isn't that an ocean?)

"Your first task," inform your students, "will be to write an alphabetized list of 100 adjectives that best describe you. You may use your own

vocabulary, your friends' and family members' suggestions, and a thesaurus to help you locate some of the expensive and confusing words."

Explain the second part of the activity by stating that no one becomes who they are all on their own; throughout your life, people influence your personality, likes and dislikes, self-confidence, and so on. Friends, teachers, family: they help shape the person you grow to become.

Next, share Chester's story about his grandmother, reading it aloud. Ask students to find some words on Chester's list that he might attribute to his grandmother's influence. "It will be your job to find someone in *your* life who has been as influential to you as Chester's grandmother was to him. Then, you will compose a brief essay describing this person's impact on you."

Instead of telling your students what the third part of this activity entails, simply show them the rocking chair concrete poem (page 109) that Chester created out of his adjectives. Be prepared for *oohs* and *aahs* as students react to this visual. Point out to them that most of the adjectives are found within the chair itself, while a few others serve as a "frame" for the artwork—which they may also do. (Some especially astute students may notice that even the words in Chester's chair are alphabetized!) Their task? Create a visual symbol, in adjectives, that represents some aspect of the essay they just wrote.

If you wish, you may also share the other student sample provided with this lesson, since it gives an array of different responses to the same prompt.

3. Invite Students to Complete Their Own Responses

Distribute the "W-A-A-A-A-Y Beyond Description" instruction sheet to each student, so it can serve as a reminder to students of the tasks ahead of them.

Usually, students can get most of their adjectives selected during the initial class period devoted to this activity. You may allow time in class the next day to finish this as well as to work on first drafts of the essays, or you may have students do these exclusively at home. Regardless, be sure to allow time during class for revision of essays and concrete poems. Have students read each other's work, asking for clarity and further details and offering other suggestions as they see fit.

Note: To help students figure out what to look for when giving each other suggestions for revision, share Chester's essay once again and ask for specific comments regarding what makes it an effective piece of writing and where it could have been improved.

Encourage students to make their concrete poems large enough so that the words are legible. Also encourage the use of thin-lined markers or black ink to help with this. Remind students that their concrete poem should be made up of most, if not all, of the 100 adjectives they have selected. In our use, we have found that some students draw a picture and then add the words around the picture. This might be acceptable for younger students, but the "power" of the image gets minimized when this is done.

When the project is complete, display the concrete poems, essays, and word lists in a triangular pattern. In the middle of the triangle, place a headshot photo of the student author. If wall space is an issue, display several projects at a time, changing them weekly, or post them on a class website or blog.

Extensions

Classroom Extensions

1. Invite students to be creative in their word selection. If they are studying a foreign language, have them locate some adjectives in that language. If they enjoy anime, have them find a few Japanese words that can be added to their word lists. Also, allow your students to invent some of their own adjectives—for example, "snail-like." (You might want to limit the invented adjectives to ten.)

2. If the person who the student highlights is still alive, have him or her write to this person, enclosing or attaching a copy of the completed project. This can be one of the most beneficial parts of this activity, as the coach, grandparent, friend, or former teacher who receives this gift will cherish it. If the person is no longer alive, send a copy of this project to a family member or close friend who knew this individual.

3. Tell students they can find new adjectives while helping the poor; have them visit www.freerice.com. This website, designed by a father to help his son study vocabulary in advance of taking the Scholastic Aptitude Test (SAT), donates 20 grains of rice to a developing country for every right answer students get to a vocabulary quiz. To date, billions of grains of rice have been distributed worldwide.

School Extension

This is one of the best activities we have found to do with an entire team or grade level. Teachers who participate should complete this project with their students and, once finished, hold a grade-level celebration of the results.

Family Extension

If you do this activity near the end of the school year, you may be able to use the results as a present for either Mother's Day or Father's Day. Instead of telling the students to pick anyone for the essay portion of the project, direct them to select a parent (or someone who has served them as a parent). It will be a gift that is never thrown away.

W-A-A-A-A-A-Y Beyond Description

Instruction Sheet

No one else in the world is exactly like you, and, until cloning becomes common, that is the way it will be. But you have become the person you are thanks to others in your life—family, friends, teachers, strangers, even book characters! This activity will help you examine who you are and the influences that helped create that person. It has three parts.

Part 1.

Find 100 adjectives that describe you and list them alphabetically. Try to find new and interesting words—as long as you learn what they mean.

Part 2.

Complete a short essay (200–400 words) describing both an *individual* and an *incident* that helped form the person you are today. In effect, this essay will explain how you became the adjectives you chose to describe yourself in Part 1.

Part 3.

This is the most revealing, creative, and interpretative part of this assignment: take all 100 adjectives (or as many as you can fit) and create an illustration *using only these adjectives*. This illustration, called a concrete poem, will relate in some symbolic way to the essay you have written. For example, you might create an image of a **tree**, because the person you wrote about shared her love of nature with you. Maybe it will be a **spiral**, because the person you wrote about enters and re-enters your life occasionally, always leaving an impression on you. Whatever you decide, no drawing is wrong if it depicts *your* life, as you see it.

Think deeply, and have a good trip!

Vocabulary Quiz

So, are you . . .

ebullient or dour?

Loquacious or Taciturn?

PERSPICACIOUS or Naïve?

Unostentatious or Vainglorious?

Monochromatic or Motley?

Lackadaisical or Emulous?

W-A-A-A-A-Y Beyond Description

Sample Student Response, *Chester, 8th grade*

Grandmother

The person who has influenced me the most is my grandmother. She is a very devout Buddhist. Back in Taiwan, we often played at home, and she often took my sister and me to Buddhist temples. She is always the one organizing the Buddhist rituals at home and the one who seems to know everything. She showed me quite a few rituals, and because of her commitment to being a Buddhist, I was exposed to Buddhism at a very young age.

In Taiwan, we had a rocking chair. When I was five, my family bought that rocking chair. I do not remember how much I liked it, but my parents told me that both my sister and I were always fighting to play with the chair. I was younger, so normally I was the one who got to play in the chair first. It was quite a big chair for me at the time, but as I grew older, the chair seemed smaller and smaller.

The thing I remember most about that chair is that on the days my sister went to school, I was alone with my grandmother. In the afternoons, my grandmother would hold me in that rocking chair and tell me religious stories. It was so comfortable, and that is why I have only heard a few endings to her stories. I often fell asleep before my grandmother could finish her stories. Now, whenever I see rocking chairs, I think of my grandmother holding me, telling me stories.

Active	Decorous	Jovial	Pacific	Sincere
Adaptable	Delighted	Kind	Patient	Smart
Admirable	Devout	Kindhearted	Patriotic	Spirited
Adventurous	Energetic	Knowing	Persistent	Steady
Amiable	Engaging	Lawful	Perspicacious	Strict
Ample	Entertaining	Liberal	Pietistic	Strong
Anxious	Ethical	Lively	Pious	Stubborn
Attractive	Fair	Lonely	Powerful	Successful
Benevolent	Fascinating	Lonesome	Quick	Superior
Brave	Fortunate	Loquacious	Quiet	Symbiotic
Brilliant	Generous	Loving	Reasonable	Talkative
Capable	Gentle	Mature	Religious	Thoughtful
Caring	Guileless	Modest	Resistant	Traditional
Cheerful	Gullible	Moral	Resolute	Understanding
Clever	Happy	Munificent	Respectable	Unselfish
Compassionate	Healthy	Nervous	Respectful	Unsparing
Conscientious	Honest	Nice	Reverent	Virtuous
Conservative	Inflexible	Noble	Saving	Vivacious
Courteous	Intelligent	Obstinate	Sensible	Wealthy
Cute	Interesting	Old	Shy	Wise

continued →

STEADY, STRICT, STRONG, STUBBORN, SUCCESSFUL, SUPERIOR, SYMPATHETIC, TALKATIVE, THOUGHTFUL, TRADITIONAL, UNDERSTANDING, UNSELFISH

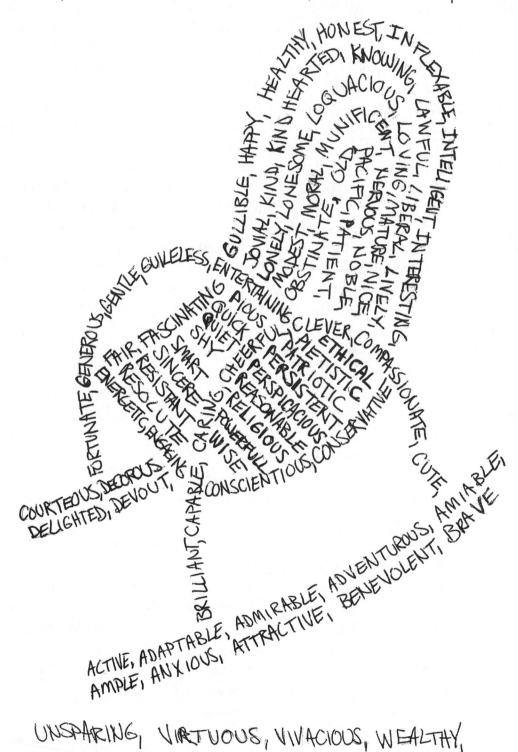

UNSPARING, VIRTUOUS, VIVACIOUS, WEALTHY, RESPECTABLE, RESPECTFUL, REVERENT, SAVING, SENSIBLE, SPIRITED

W-A-A-A-A-A-Y Beyond Description
Sample Student Response, *Seth, 8th grade*

From Cousin to Hero

We ended with a final bow, everyone in synchronization. I went to see my family, get their congratulations, hug and kiss them, you know. As I saw who was there to greet me, a smile came to my face. It was my mom, grandma, grandpa . . . and my cousin, Jackie. Jackie is 14 years old and already more accomplished than I may ever be. She's won a gold medal in the Olympics and is currently a star of her softball team, among many other things. She came up to me and gave me a hug. Then she held my hand as we walked around and talked to the cast members.

After about 20 minutes or so, my family got ready to leave. I walked them to their car, saying good-bye. To my surprise, before getting in, Jackie gave me a big hug. This made me feel special, so I gave her a rose of mine that I had received from a cast mate.

My grandparents later told me that Jackie held that rose all the way home, saying things like, "I want to be in a play! I want to be like Seth!" Well, everyone needs someone to look up to, right? Absolutely . . . except I don't think Jackie ever had before that night. You see, Jackie has autism, disabling her from doing many things a lot of other people can do. Her gold medal was for ice skating in the Special Olympics. The award was for high accomplishments of a child with a disability.

For Jackie to admire and congratulate me is an unexplainable feeling. Sure, we may not have ever had an actual conversation . . . but just a hug from her alone is a conversation worth a million words. Jackie still has her rose, frail and withered, yet still beautiful. I guess she's just living proof that the predators don't always win.

Thanks, Jackie, you're a star! Don't be afraid to shine!

Accepting	Crazy	Frivolous	Loco	Pompous	Subarashii**
Action-packed	Curious	Fun	Lofty	Pulchritudinous	Suteki**
Aimable*	Delicious	Funny	Loquacious	Religious	Sympathetique*
Alluring	Disney-loving	Gawky	Lovey-dovey	Respectful	Ticklish
Animated	Ditzy	Giddy	Ludicrous	Rhythmic	Truthful
Astral	Dramatic	Groovy	Made-to-order	Righteous	Undeniable
Audacious	Duplicitous	Gullible	Majestic	Rollicking	Unforgettable
Beefheaded	Duteous	Happy	Mellifluous	Romanesque	Vainglorious
Brave	Elaborate	Heteroclitic	Mischievous	Salubrious	Vociferous
Brilliant	Elastic	Hotchpotch	Naïve	Saucy	Wacky
Bumfuzzled	Endurable	Hunky-dory	Necromantic	Self-righteous	Warm-hearted
Capricious	Extravagant	Impassible	Okashi**	Semi-egotistical	Whippy
Childish	Exuberant	Irresistible	Open	Silly	Wild
Chowchow	Faithful	Jolly	Optimistic	Slick	Zany
Christian	Feckful	Ki no kuratta**	Outgoing	Smiley	
Comique*	Foolish	Kooky	Passionate	Spunky	* = French
Congenial	Friendly	Lickety-split	Pell-mell	Steadfast	** = Japanese

continued →

From *Building Strong Writers in Middle School: Classroom-Ready Activities That Inspire Creativity and Support Core Standards* by Deb Delisle and Jim Delisle, copyright © 2011. Free Spirit Publishing Inc., Minneapolis, MN; 800-735-7323; www.freespirit.com. This page may be reproduced for use within an individual school or district. For all other uses, contact www.freespirit.com/company/permissions.cfm.

17. A Case of Vowel Play

This activity began when a student surprised us with an exceptional book report that she had done in a challenging way. Jordan, a seventh grader with strong skills in writing, had just read a book she enjoyed, *The Red Badge of Courage,* and decided to write her review of this book in an intriguing manner: The entire book report would be written without using the letter "e."

There were, of course, two problems with this idea: first, the book's title contains several e's; second, the main character's name is Henry. She gave herself permission to use both the book's title and its main character's name in her report, and then began her otherwise-*e*-less report. Here is an excerpt from Jordan's work:

"*The Red Badge of Courage* is about a young man's trip from acting in ways of a coward to acting in ways of a strong, audacious army man. A youth, Henry joins army ranks with aspirations of coming out daring and valiant. Soon, though, Henry finds out that actual war contains complications his thoughts did not contain in his original analysis. . . ."

More than 500 *e*-free words later, Jordan had a book report—among the most thoughtful and precise we have ever read. Looking exhausted and spent as she turned in her project, Jordan admitted (grudgingly) that this report, though difficult to complete, was one of her most engaging assignments ever. Why? Because Jordan had stretched herself to her language arts limits—and she emerged victorious. For the first time in a long time, Jordan didn't just *get* an "A," she *earned* one.

So, of course, we began to think immediately about extending this assignment into another dimension. The end result: "A Case of Vowel Play," an activity that serves dual purposes: First, it helps middle school students enhance their written and verbal communication skills, and second, it connects your students with younger ones, who often look up to older kids as role models.

Product	Illustrated books that students make in small groups, in which a vowel is missing from the story and the text for an extended section; this book will then be read to kindergarten or first-grade children
Materials	• 1 display copy of the "Thngs y knw mtchng clmn" activity sheet (page 116) • 1 copy of the "A Case of Vowel Play" handout (page 117) for each student • Several thesauruses (hard copies or online versions, such as www.merriam-webster.com) • 7–8 large pieces of poster board for each book's cover and pages • Yarn or ribbon • A variety of crayons and colored pencils • 1 evaluation form for each book that is created
Time	Five to six 45-minute class periods to introduce and begin the project, and to allow groups time to plan their stories, write and illustrate their books, and share them with younger students. You may want to assign portions of this project for homework, although, as a group project, that could be a problem for students unable to gather in a common place after school.
Common Core State Standards	Activity meets standards 1–4, 6, 7, 12, 14, 15, 16, and 19 from the chart on page 5.

Activity Steps

1. The Hook

Begin the lesson by having the following message written on the board as the students arrive for class:

"Wlcm stdnts! W'r ll n fr n xctng dy!"

It probably won't take long for the students to figure out this vowel-less message ("Welcome, students! We're all in for an exciting day!"). After they decipher it, display the "Thngs y knw mtchng clmn," asking for individual students to figure out which consonant pairs go together to match common titles or phrases. (Here is the solution: Pizza with pepperoni; Diary of Anne Frank; Los Angeles, California; Harry Potter; macaroni and cheese; South Pole; Walt Disney World; Dr. Seuss.)

Explain the importance of those five (or six) vowels to our written language: without them, our language would be difficult to read and almost impossible to speak. Next, ask students to write out their entire first, middle, and last names, determining which vowel is most frequent. Ask them to write an answer to this question without using that vowel: "In what ways is a six-year-old different from someone your age?"

After they have answered this question and commented on the ease or difficulty in doing so, tell them that this project will involve vowels, picture books, and six-year-olds excited to learn about both.

2. Introduce the Activity

Explain to your students what they are going to do: write and illustrate a children's book that they will share with five- or six-year-old students. The basic plot of the story will be the same for everyone: a vowel goes missing and then is found. On the pages when the vowel is missing, that vowel cannot be used in the text. Each group can decide how their vowel goes missing and how it is found.

Distribute the "A Case of Vowel Play" handout and go through it together. The handout contains the specifics of the project—the book's length, how the left-out vowel is chosen, how the students should work together to create the story, characters, and artwork, and so on. After you've reviewed the handout and answered any questions, put your students into groups of three or four.

Note: This activity requires the full cooperation of each team member. Therefore, it's important that you carefully select the members of each group, looking for combinations of students who can work well together. Emphasize to your students the importance of cooperation and full participation by everyone, especially if you are going to assign out-of-class time to complete the books. Let them know, too, that you may intervene should it become obvious to you (or made obvious to you by another student) that someone is not applying full effort to the project. We don't like to overdo the "read 'em the riot act" scene, but for the sake of this project's success, this might be a time we advise you to make an exception.

Try to make this a true group effort in every way, with each group member contributing to the plot, character development, writing, and illustration—if not equally, then close to it. Often, a student who is particularly adept at drawing will be "recruited" to be the book's sole illustrator, but this project works best when every group member carries a substantive share of the responsibility for (and pride in) every facet of the project.

3. Invite Students to Complete Their Own Responses

Now that your students are in their groups and you've covered the basics, have them figure out what vowel will go missing in their stories by writing down each group member's first, middle, and last name and determining the most common vowel in the string of names. That will be their missing vowel.

Next, give them time to start brainstorming the basics of their storybook. Remind them that their audience is going to be kindergartners and first graders, so keep those young kids in mind when working. Here are some guidelines you may want to offer to help them begin:

1. Select a setting that young children would know—playgrounds, schools, shopping malls, amusement parks, etc.

2. Suggest that each group member choose a character and develop that character's personality. Perhaps one will be the "funny" character while another is the character who always worries about the lost vowel. Yet another might be an adult character, while a fourth might be the one who always thinks of a possible solution to the problem of finding the missing vowel.

3. Suggest that students outline their plot before they begin writing. Specifically: how does the vowel go missing, where does it go, what is it doing while the other alphabet letters are searching for it. Also, how do the other characters notice it is gone? How do they go about searching for it? How do they find it?

Once the students have a general idea of their story and its characters, ask them to check in with you to explain how they plan to proceed. It is not essential that your students know every single detail of the story at this point—those will emerge as they write—but they should be able to identify the characters, setting, and overall sequence of their story.

Also—again keeping their young readers in mind—remind students that when the particular vowel character disappears, it cannot be due to anything violent. No kidnappings allowed! Instead, the vowel could disappear to its bedroom to read a book, or to the school nurse's office to fix a scraped knee, or to an amusement park to watch the cotton candy machine spin its sugary concoction! It's best that when the vowel eventually gets "found" near the end of the book, that it is not crying and upset at having been separated; rather, it was just off by itself, feeling safe. With very young children, a happy ending is a good way to end any book.

After the students have met with you to review their story plans, give each group a copy of the "Evaluation Form." This is the form that students from your class will use to assess each group's book and can serve as a useful guide to writing an engaging story. Encourage your students to refer to this sheet as they develop their book.

Give groups time each day to work on their books. You may find it useful to have each group give a brief overview to the class on where they are in terms of its completion, especially if they are having trouble getting started or hitting a "creative snag." Another helpful idea is to have groups visit other groups to compare and gather ideas. Also, keep referring your students back to the evaluation form, which can help them focus on improving each element of their books. The more specific they can be about the snags they are facing, the more likely it will be that their classmates (or you) can help them move forward in their book's creation.

Here are some other helpful guidelines:

• Write and draw words and illustrations in pencil first. They should ink their words and color in their drawings as the book nears completion and they are satisfied with the content.

• Check spelling, grammar, and mechanics before inking the words.

• Check the illustrations for consistency before coloring them in. (For example, if the book's plot takes place in one day, the colors on the characters' clothes should be the same throughout the book.)

There will be design flaws and errors made. That's okay. Remind your students that most six-year-olds are very forgiving, especially when older kids come to their classroom to share some time and books with them.

4. Share the Books

The culminating event is traveling to a nearby primary school (or within your own school if it includes younger grades) where the new authors in your class read their books to small groups of kindergarten or first-grade students. We suggest using two or three classrooms where each of your student groups reads their book to two or three groups of young students per classroom, in a round-robin format. This will allow your students to see how different children interpret and enjoy their work and will serve as a great basis of discussion when your students compare how the same "lesson" went over from one group of young children to the next.

Extensions

Classroom Extensions

1. Bring a digital camera to your classroom visits and take photos of your students reading their books to the young students. A day or two after your students have read their books to the younger ones, distribute the photos and have your students write comments about what they thought of the experience on a piece of lined paper attached to each photo. As one of our eighth-graders said:

> *Reading our handmade book with the first graders not only was fun, but it made me proud of my group's hard work. The young children loved the book as much as we did. They all listened attentively and asked questions with enthusiasm. First graders are very smart for their age! They all wanted to read our book out loud!*

Alternatively, you could paste the photos into a blog post about the project and invite students to comment—including the younger students who were visited.

2. Make an extra copy of each of the photos and ask your students to write thank-you messages to the kindergartners and first-grade students. Make sure that you have a photo of each group, though, on the day of the readings—no one wants to be left out!

3. Share with your students copies of *The Vowel Family: A Tale of Lost Letters* (Sally M. Walker, 2008) or *Elemenopee: The Day L-M-N-O-and P Left the Alphabet* (Paula Hall, 2003). Both picture books deal with the same "loss" of vowels in interesting ways. *Elemenopee* is a pop-up book that might inspire one or more of your groups to attempt a similar book.

School Extension

On page 112, we mentioned Jordan, a seventh grader who wrote a book report without using the letter "e." You and your teaching colleagues might consider a similar project for your own students, assigning an activity in a variety of subjects—a book report for language arts, a biography of a historical figure for social studies, a science lab report—in which a particular alphabet letter is missing. Once these projects are completed, they may be displayed under signs that read "What . . . no 'A'?" or "What . . . no 'I'?" An activity like this helps in building vocabulary, as students must find synonyms for words that contain their forbidden vowel. Also, those thesauruses that have been used sparingly will get good use as students seek new words to tell their tales.

Family Extension

Invite your students to bring their books home and read them to younger siblings, cousins, or neighbors. Might as well spread the wealth when the wealth is this good!

Thngs y knw mtchng clmn

Pzz wth . . .   nn Frnk

Dry f . . .   Wrld

Ls ngls . . .   Pttr

Hrr . . .   ppprn

Mcrn . . .   Pl

Sth . . .   Ss

Wlt Dsn . . .   Clfrn

Dr . . .   nd chs

A Case of Vowel Play

Though there are only five of them (or six, if you count *y*), what would the English language do without them?

Without what?

Why, vowels, of course—those little letters that make a "cake" out of a "ck" and "energy" out of "nrg."

But something hrrbl (er . . . *horrible*) has happened! In a major case of "vowel play," one of our alphabet's most prominent members is missing. What happened? How will the missing vowel be found again? Well, that's up to you.

Together with two or three other students, you are going to write and illustrate a picture book about the missing vowel and share it with younger students.

Guidelines

1. To determine which vowel will disappear from the pages of your book, write down every group member's first, middle, and last name and determine which vowel is used most often in your combined names. That's your missing vowel.

2. The book should be 16 pages, with each page having at least one illustration.

3. You may use all the 26 alphabet letters for the first three pages of the book, but on page four, your vowel disappears! On pages 4–13, your characters search for the missing vowel—*but you cannot use this letter at any time on pages 4–13!* So, if your missing vowel is "e," you cannot use any e's on pages 4–13. Then, on pages 14–16, all the alphabet is together again and you can use all 26 letters.

4. You'll need a title and cover design (you can use any of the alphabet letters for your title).

Suggestions and Hints

1. Work out some plot ideas for your story *before* you write it. Sketch out the words and illustrations on separate sheets of paper.

2. Limit your book's characters to the number of people in your group—plus one (the missing vowel). It can be fun, and in the spirit of the project, if your characters have names that feature a letter. For example, if your name is Maria, you might create a character called "The Divine Miss M." If your name is Joe, you could create one called "Dr. J."

3. Keep a dictionary and thesaurus nearby. They'll help you find synonyms for words that do not contain your missing vowel (like "speedy" instead of "fast," if you can't use the letter "a").

4. Remember that your audience is five to seven years old. Use humor and mystery, but no violence.

5. Write no more than three sentences per page and keep the language simple enough that little kids would understand it.

6. Before you begin writing or drawing, figure out the basic plot of your story, especially the reason why your vowel has disappeared. Did it get angry with another letter and run away? Did it have a party to go to and forgot to tell the other letters? Do the other characters find the vowel, or does it return on its own? Once you have the basic outline down, it will be easier to begin writing scenes.

To keep everyone involved and interested, split up the duties equally. Let everyone write at least a few pages, and let everyone illustrate several pages, too.

And above all, have fun!

From *Building Strong Writers in Middle School: Classroom-Ready Activities That Inspire Creativity and Support Core Standards* by Deb Delisle and Jim Delisle, copyright © 2011. Free Spirit Publishing Inc., Minneapolis, MN; 800-735-7323; www.freespirit.com. This page may be reproduced for use within an individual school or district. For all other uses, contact www.freespirit.com/company/permissions.cfm.

A Case of Vowel Play
Evaluation Form

Rate each section from 1 to 5, with 5 being the highest score. Please be honest in your responses, and please provide specific comments. (For example, "Your main character has a funny personality" is better than saying, "I like your characters.")

Book's title_____

_____

Book's authors_____

_____

Your name_____

_____

The book's storyline

Is this story easy to follow? Does it have a beginning, middle, and end? Does each character have a role to play in the story? Do the ideas seem original?

1   **2**   **3**   **4**   **5**

Comments:

_____

_____

_____

_____

The book's illustrations

Are the illustrations carefully and completely drawn or designed? Do the illustrations match the story? Do the illustrations add fun to the story?

1   **2**   **3**   **4**   **5**

Comments:

_____

_____

_____

_____

The book's appeal to young children

If you were six years old, would you like to read this book or have it read to you? Would you understand the story? Would you enjoy the characters?

1   **2**   **3**   **4**   **5**

Comments:

_____

_____

_____

_____

The book's grammar and punctuation

Does the book contain complete sentences? Are rules of grammar and punctuation followed? Is spelling accurate?

1   **2**   **3**   **4**   **5**

Comments:

_____

_____

_____

_____

Overall impressions of the book

In one or two sentences, state your opinions on the overall quality of the book—the parts you liked, the parts you found confusing, and any special features of the book that will make it appeal to young children.

_____

_____

_____

_____

Writing to
Create Art

Quick! Name something that is *not* a form of art. Although most people would probably agree that a painting on a wall qualifies as art, as do a sculpted bronze statue or a mobile hanging from a museum's ceiling, what about a cartoon—is it art? Or how about a 1965 Ford Mustang? Or a perfectly cooked lasagna? A song lyric? A flawless floor exercise in gymnastics? The old expression that "beauty is in the eye of the beholder" rings true. One person's throwaway etching could be another person's masterpiece.

In compiling the writing activities for this section, we ran into this same difficulty of personal definition. In saying these activities are designed to "create art," we do not assume that all of us agree on what constitutes art. But it is the *intentions* behind art that are important here. Generally, people create art in order to prod people's thoughts or emotions, or both. When people examine a piece of art, they tend to have reactions to it: they like it (or not); they understand it (or not); they are attracted to explore it further (or not); they may be led to feel or think about things in a new way (or not).

The activities in this section urge students to try to make products others will like, or love, or think are beautiful; that lead readers (and the student-authors themselves) to think or feel something different; that will attract people to take a second look. Our students have enjoyed the following activities and created amazing writing samples that ranged from "the world's shortest essays" to blues poems rich in heart and humor, and we believe your students will, too.

Learning Objectives

- To provide opportunities for students to complement their written work with visual formats that represent the messages of their writing

- To encourage the creation of written products that will be shared with various audiences beyond the classroom

- To create written projects in a variety of unusual formats that reveal the diverse methods that can be used to express oneself to others

18. Fib's Follies

This lesson began when a teacher shared with us a poem one of her high school students had written for a class assignment. What was unusual, though, was that the poetry-sharing teacher was teaching precalculus! Who knew that math and poetry had anything in common? Here is an excerpt from that teacher's letter:

"When I was teaching sequences, I did some research on the Internet and came across some Fibonacci poetry, so I gave the assignment of writing a Fibonacci poem for extra credit. I was overwhelmed by what my tenth graders turned in to me."

For those of you who are math savvy, the Fibonacci sequence is generated by this rule:

$$F_n = F_{n-1} + F_{n-2}$$

For the math phobic, or for those who have only a fuzzy recollection of anything beyond long division, the Fibonacci sequence is a pattern that has been called "nature's numbering system." You encounter the Fibonacci sequence every day, as it appears naturally in the petals of flowers, the spirals of pinecones, and the scales on pineapples.

Product	A collection of poems written in a specific way that mimics the mathematical phenomenon of the Fibonacci sequence
Materials	• 1 display copy of the "I Hope You See . . ." poem (page 124) • 1 copy of "Fibonacci Poetry" handout (page 125) for each student • 1 display copy of "The Mystery of the Fib." (page 126) • Optional: 1 pineapple, some marigolds, a pinecone, black-eyed Susans, or sunflowers (photos of these items will also work: do an Internet image search for "Fibonacci sequence in nature")
Time	One 45-minute class period to explain the lesson and begin some writing, with homework to complete the assignment (or additional class time if preferred)
Common Core State Standards	Activity meets standards 2, 3, 4, 6, 12, and 14–19 from the chart on page 5.

Activity Steps

1. The Hook

Ask your students to ponder the following idealized situation: "Suppose a newly born pair of rabbits, one male and one female, is put in a field. Rabbits are able to mate at the age of one month [pause here for student gasps!], and once conceived, new rabbits are born in one month. At the end of the second month, a female can produce another pair of rabbits. Suppose that these rabbits **never die** and that the female **always** produces one new pair (male and female) from the second month on. How many pairs of rabbits will there be in a year?"

Of course, your students may remind you that you have forgotten the fact that you teach language arts, not math. Remind them (smugly, of course) that you will get there soon enough.

The answer to the above rabbit population boom is as follows, which you can illustrate if none of your students has beaten you to it.

1. At the end of the first month, the rabbits mate, but there is still only one pair.

2. At the end of the second month, the female produces a new pair, so there are now two pairs of rabbits in the field.

3. At the end of the third month, the original female produces a second pair, making three pairs in the field.

4. At the end of the fourth month, the original female has produced yet another new pair, while the female born two months ago produces her first pair, making five pairs of rabbits.

5. The sequence continues as such. The number of pairs of rabbits in the field at the start of each month is as follows: 1, 1, 2, 3, 5, 8, 13, 21, 34, 55, 89, 144. So, by December's end, the field will be hopping with 144 pairs of bunnies.

Astute students will realize the simplicity of the above sequence: the way to get to the new number is to add the two preceding numbers. Thus, $1 + 1 = 2$, $2 + 1 = 3$, $3 + 2 = 5$ and so on, until $55 + 89 = 144$. The sequence is endless.

End this introduction by displaying the "I Hope You See . . ." poem, which is written using the Fibonacci sequence with respect to each line's syllable count.

2. Introduce the Activity

Now that you have totally inspired and impressed your students with your blending of mathematics and writing, it's time to turn them on to another subject: science. If you brought in the optional fruit and flowers to show as examples, take these out for display and close inspection. If not, show photos you've found online that show the Fibonacci sequence.

Time after time the Fibonacci sequence appears in nature. For example, a sunflower spirals out from its center in both a clockwise and a counterclockwise direction, and the number of spirals is always two consecutive numbers in the Fibonacci sequence. The same is true in pine cones, where the spirals start at the cone's base and go round and round the side until reaching the cone's top—all in numbers that fall into the Fibonacci sequence. The same patterns are found in the shells of snails and in countless other instances in nature. After explaining and showing your students these patterns, allow them to examine your examples.

Let your students know that they are going to write poetry in which the syllables adhere to the Fibonacci sequence. Specifically, the first two lines of their poem will consist of one syllable each, the third line will contain two syllables, the fourth line three syllables . . . and on and on, just as in the example that you read to them to introduce this activity.

If you're so inclined, after dazzling your students with your knowledge of writing, mathematics, *and* science, you can offer them another lesson . . . in history:

Leonardo Fibonacci of Pisa lived from 1170–1250 and is considered by many to be the greatest mathematician of the Middle Ages. Even though the sequence is named after him, Fibonacci did not discover the above sequence, which had, indeed, been noticed by Indian mathematicians as early as the sixth century. However, in a book that Fibonacci wrote in the thirteenth century, he introduced Europeans to the Hindu-Arabic numeral system (which uses the numerals 0–9 and place values), focusing on how this system could be useful for bookkeeping, weights and measures, calculating interest, and other mathematical operations we perform every day. He also mentioned in an "oh, by the way" manner that a curious sequence of numbers appeared in nature frequently. Ever since then, this sequence has been associated with the mathematician who introduced the concept to the Western world.

3. Invite Students to Complete Their Own Responses

Distribute the "Fibonacci Poetry" handout to your students and go over it together. Focus your students' attention on the bottom of the page, where the assignment specifications are detailed. The topics listed are meant as starting points only; invite your students to come up with additional ideas for prompts. You may require as many Fib sequence poems as you wish.

To help your students get a stronger grasp on the assignment, distribute "The Mystery of the Fib.," written by Nadine, an eighth grader in Texas. As her teacher explained to us, "Nadine's poem overwhelmed me in so many ways—four stanzas; the sequence reversing; but mostly it was the content. *Wow!*"

We certainly agree! Suggest to your students that they, too, could use an increasing and decreasing line length (reversing the sequence).

There should be some time during this class session for your students to select a topic for their poems and begin writing the initial lines or stanzas. Ask students to complete their poems at home that night and bring in their creations the next day, when you can have them read each other's work and offer each other ideas and tips for revision. Post the finished results in or outside of your classroom or on a class website or blog, preferably attached to a photo that was taken or downloaded of an aspect of nature that follows the Fibonacci sequence.

Extensions

Classroom Extensions

1. If students need to complete book reports or character studies, have them write these assignments using a Fib sequence structure.

2. If students who are more mathematically or scientifically inclined would like to pursue further research on the Fibonacci sequence, ask them to explore "The Mystery of the Golden Ratio" (readily accessible on many websites, especially as it relates to the human body). Among other things, your students will discover that the following ratios are all identical:

- between the length and width of one's face
- between the length of one's mouth to the width of one's nose
- the distance between the shoulder line and the top of the head

All these ratios are 1: 1.618—the exact ratio that makes the basis for the Fibonacci sequence.

School Extension

Many schools celebrate "Pi Day" in mid-March, to celebrate the magic and mystery of the number pi. Why not *also* have a "Fib Day," during which students recite their Fib sequence poetry, display artwork and photography they have created using the Fib sequence, create and play board games where moves can only be made sequentially according to the Fib sequence, and search the school grounds for examples of the Fib sequence in nature? As icing on the cake, ask one of the math teachers to dress up as Leonardo Fibonacci and detail some of his other mathematical ideas and discoveries. End the day with a game show, "The biggest Fib-ber," in which students tell one truth and one lie about anything mathematical, while the audience tries to figure out which is which.

Family Extension

Students and their parents can search for the Fib sequence in a variety of forms, including the following:

- In art: Leonardo da Vinci used the Fib sequence in some of his paintings, including *The Annunciation*.
- In movies: *The Da Vinci Code* uses the Fib sequence as a safe's combination.
- In music: Artists as diverse as Tool in "Lateralus" and Claude Debussy in "Reflections in Water" use the Fib sequence in their songs' rhythms.
- In architecture: The Parthenon in Athens and the United Nations Building in New York City both use the Fib sequence in some aspects of their design.
- In nature: Nothing like a good walk outside to reveal nature's many examples of the Fib sequence.

Further, an online search for "Fibonacci games" will provide many examples of easy-to-difficult puzzles that use the Fib sequence for reaching a solution.

I
Hope
You see
The beauty
And timeless wonder
Of the Fibonacci sequence

Because this is going to be your next assignment

Fibonacci Poetry

The Fibonacci sequence is nature's numbering system. Time and time again, a plant's leaves or an animal's scales are arranged in this sequence. So, the number of bracts on a pinecone or the arrangement of scales on a pineapple are similar from one pineapple or pinecone to the next. The Fibonacci sequence was discovered centuries ago and, as you'll soon learn, it applies to many objects in nature.

In the Fibonacci sequence, each number is the sum of the two preceding numbers, like this: 1, 1, 2, 3, 5, 8, 13, 21, 34, 55, 89, 144, 377, 610, 987, 1597, 2584, 4181 . . . (each succeeding number is the sum of the previous two).

Just as the Fibonacci sequence creates beauty in nature, so can it create beauty in art. Your assignment is to use this rhythmic pattern in the lines of a poem.

Take a look at the following examples. The first line of each poem is just one syllable, as is the second line. Each poem's third line is two syllables, and each poem's fourth line is three syllables. The number of syllables in each line corresponds to the numbers in the Fibonacci sequence.

One
Small
Precise
Poetic
Spiraling mixture
Math plus poetry yields the Fib

Math
makes
my head
quake with pain.
Writing a poem based
on Fibonacci does the same

This
Is
Far more
Geeky than
Another haiku
Can't we just forget the whole thing?

This
is
going
to be a
terrible poem
unless I nail a great finish

Here are some ideas for topics, but you may also come up with your own:

- I learned this about myself as a student . . .
- I cope with stress by . . .
- When I want to change things in my life, I will . . .
- I have discovered that I need . . .
- I have discovered that I love . . .
- I'd like my teachers (or parents or friends, etc.) to know . . .
- When I think of a memory I want to keep forever . . .
- My life's biggest goals involve . . .
- What is better than . . .

Your poem does not have to rhyme (none of the examples do), and it's up to you to make it either profound and insightful or playful and humorous—a lot of that depends on which of the above prompts you select.

Now.
Get
To work.
You have no
Time to sit and sit
While other students are writing!

The Mystery of the Fib.

by Nadine, 8th grade

I

love

it when

I'm able

to bring together

my artistry and nerdiness

universally

united

nature

and

math

And

yet

is this

but one great

coincidence that

Fib's sequence can be found in things

from flowers to bees

that do not

comply

to

math?

Will

we

ever

discover

if Fibonacci

uncovered the numbers that could

provide the bridge for

the worlds of

nature

and

math?

Or

do

answers

to questions

of such magnitude

remain as mysteries to us.

the idea that

nature could

answer

to

math?

19. It's All Greek
(or Latin, or Arabic . . .) to Me

The English language is a polyglot: a mishmash of words stolen and borrowed from other, older languages as diverse as Latin, Greek, Sanskrit, and Chinese. Of course, many of our students are unaware of how much the English language overlaps these foreign tongues, but every time they pet their **poodle** (German), reach for the **ketchup** (Chinese), or unpack their **trombone** (Italian), they are using words from (or rooted in) a foreign tongue.

In this activity, students get introduced to some of the thousands of words that were "borrowed" countless years ago in distant lands before they became essential elements in the language we speak every day. As they build their vocabularies, they also get to have a little fun creating "foreign" sentences that have English written all over them.

Ready for a **lesson** (French) that has **zero** (Arabic) level of **tedium** (Latin)? *Voilà!* (French, of course!)

Product	Individual, illustrated posters containing sentences composed of words derived from other languages
Materials	• Access to one or more of the websites Online Etymology Dictionary (www.etymonline.com) and KryssTal Borrowed Words in English (www.krysstal.com/borrow.html) • 1 sheet of 9" x 12" poster board per student • Various colored fine-line markers or colored pencils for all students • 1 copy of the "It's All Greek (or Latin, or Arabic . . .) to Me" handout (page 130) for each student • 1 display copy of the "Creative Constructions" handout (page 131) • 1 display copy of the examples of foreign sentences completed by sixth, seventh, and eighth graders (page 132) • 1 world map, displayed in the front of the classroom or on an interactive white board • Push pins, for use on the map (or a pointer for the white board)
Time	Two class periods: the first for students to research the etymology of particular words, and the second to compose sentences and illustrate their posters
Common Core State Standards	Activity meets standards 2, 3, 4, 6, 12, and 14–19 from the chart on page 5.

Activity Steps

1. The Hook

When students get settled into your classroom, ask if anyone speaks a different language. As they tell you which languages they can speak, write these on the board. Next, ask for several volunteers to say something in their foreign tongue, asking other class members to translate these words, phrases, and sentences into English, if they can. If no student knows the translation, ask the student who spoke the different language to translate it for the class.

As straight-faced as you can muster, let your students know that all of them speak a foreign language already—in fact, many foreign languages. "I'll prove it to you—now, answer these questions out loud as I ask them."

- "What do you say when someone sneezes?" *Gesundheit.* (After students respond, place a push pin into the country of Germany. Gesundheit means "health.")
- "What do you call the building where you park a car?" *Garage.* (Put a pin in France.)
- "What is the name of a stringed instrument you place under your chin?" *Violin.* (Put a pin in Italy.)
- "What is the name of a sour, yellow fruit that makes your mouth pucker?" *Lemon.* (Put a pin in Saudi Arabia.)
- "What is the name of the toy or tool that comes back to you after you throw it?" *Boomerang.* (Put a pin in Australia.)
- "Where would you see bucking broncos and bareback riding?" *Rodeo.* (Put a pin in Spain.)
- "What is the name of the red stuff that people put on French fries?" *Ketchup.* (Put a pin in China.)

End this question session by telling your students that they are about to explore a foreign language: English.

2. Introduce the Activity

Distribute the "It's All Greek (or Latin, or Arabic . . .) to Me" handout and review some of the words on the list, asking students if they can think of any other words that might be of foreign origin. Compile a list of these words, telling your students that you'll have a chance to look these up later using one of the websites listed at the bottom of the student handout.

Next, display the "Creative Constructions" sheet, showing one sentence at a time. You might need to explain or define some of the words, but students will likely get the general meaning of the sentences. Tell them that each word in all caps is derived from another language. Say, "Now, if you could illustrate these sentences, here's what they might look like." Show students the two illustrated samples and ask student volunteers to create a quick sketch of another of the "Creative Constructions."

Then tell your students, "Your task is to create a humorous sentence in which at least four of the words are derived from other languages, accompanied by an illustration that is a visual depiction of your sentence."

At this point, you may choose to share the handout of completed responses from sixth through eighth graders to provide more examples of how they might approach the assignment.

3. Invite Students to Complete Their Own Responses

With the remaining time left in the class period, have your students access the websites listed at the bottom of their student handout and write down some words or phrases they find that they might like to place in their original "Creative Construction," telling them to write both the *word* and its *language of origin.* Have them collect 20 or so words, which is more than they will need to use.

During the second class period, remind students of their task—to complete a sentence composed of mainly "borrowed" words and to illustrate the sentence with markers and/or colored pencils. Allow about 20 minutes for students to locate more foreign words, devoting the rest of the class period to the creation of the illustrated poster. If time allows, ask students to share their pieces with others, or simply display their work in the classroom or hallway.

Extensions

Classroom Extensions

1. Bring a bit of geography into this lesson by having students draw the national flag of the countries of origin of the words in their sentences (a credit card–sized flag works well). You could have them display the flags attached to the words with string, or have them attach this flag with a push pin onto the world map into which you'd stuck pins earlier.

2. As a class, in groups, or individually, have students do some of the activities at the alpha-Dictionary website (www.alphadictionary .com), a site that provides both informative and humorous examples of the distinctiveness of the English language. Among the activities you will find are pages of Latin and Greek root words and their influence on our language; a "Rebel/Yankee" quiz, which reveals how regional pronunciations and idioms can pinpoint pretty quickly the part of the United States where you were raised; a listing of the English language's most misspelled words (including *misspelled!);* and a "Folk Etymology" section, which details how foreign words that were difficult to pronounce were changed to accommodate our English-speaking ways—words like *artichoke, cockamamie, blunderbuss,* and other wacky words that actually have meaning in several languages. You can even learn and practice Russian grammar and vocabulary using this website.

School Extension

Take a look at how the English language continues to change and grow over time by searching the Web using the term "Oxford English Dictionary new words for 2011" (or any year you choose). You will find the top ten new words "accepted" by dictionary compilers for the first time that year. For example, here are some words newly coined in the 21st century:

2010	2009
overthink	*Muggle*
defriend	*cyberslacking*
frenemy	*prebuttal*
automagically	*threequel*
netbook	*bouncebackability*

Post these "new" words on the school's website or weekly bulletin, asking students to write their own definitions of these words that evolved from our everyday behaviors and culture. Also, ask students to suggest some additional words that should make the *Oxford English Dictionary* for the first time for the upcoming year.

Family Extension

Even if your students' parents or grandparents are not fluent in any foreign language, they may use names for family members or "terms of endearment" that reveal the family's background. For example, "Grandma" might be *grand mere* in some families with French heritage, *yiayiá* in a household of Greek heritage, and *abuela* in a home with Spanish heritage. Compile a list of these terms used in your students' families and investigate their original language sources, which are likely to relate directly to each family's heritage from several generations past. One way to do this research is by www.ask.com, posing the question "What do different cultures (or languages) call 'grandmother' (or any relative)?" This will give you some commonly used terms that may be similar to those used by your students in their families.

It's All Greek
(or Latin, or Arabic . . .) to Me

The English language has borrowed heavily from older languages that are spoken across the world. Here are just a few examples of common English words, organized by their language of origin:

Arabic: algebra, genie, lemon, magazine, mattress, sherbet, sofa, tariff, zero

Australian Aborigine: boomerang, kangaroo, koala

Chinese: gung ho, ketchup, tea

French: beret, cadet, camouflage, chef, garage, pastel, sabotage, toupee

German: delicatessen, dumb, kindergarten, nickel, quartz, waltz

Greek: circus, eureka, genesis, phobia

Hebrew: amen, cinnamon, jubilee, rabbi

Italian: balcony, balloon, bravo, pasta, studio, trombone

Japanese: kimono, soy, teriyaki, tycoon

Latin: alibi, axis, extra, integer, ratio, trivia

Sanskrit: bandana, cheetah, dungarees, polo, shampoo

Spanish: banana, canyon, cocoa, macho, poncho, rodeo, tomato, tortilla

Various Native American Languages: canoe, moccasin, moose, powwow, tomahawk

As you can see, English is like a jigsaw puzzle of other languages combined to create a new language spoken by billions of people worldwide. Called **loanwords** by those who study words for a living—*etymologists*—these borrowed words are used by people every day, in almost every sentence we speak and read. Here are two websites that will help you discover more of the meaning behind the English language:

- KryssTal Borrowed Words in English (www.krysstal.com/borrow.html). This site explores how 146 languages have given us words we use in everyday conversations and written communications.

- Online Etymology Dictionary (www.etymonline.com). Curious about a particular word's origin? Plug it into this site and you'll find out its original language and meaning.

Happy hunting as you explore the world of words!

Creative Constructions

The PHAROAH was chewing GUM and drinking TEA in the middle of a TYPHOON with a SAMURAI chasing him.

The RACCOON was in the GARAGE sticking CHOP SUEY up his nose and SHAMPOOING his hair while stepping on a SKUNK.

The AMIGO went to the FIESTA in his new MUSTANG then ate CHILI with BANANAS and had COCOA to drink.

The SWAMI was ill from eating too much MOLASSES while riding a PALOMINO in a SKIRT.

A KINDERGARTEN CHEF stuffed LEMONS into his MADRAS BANDANA and WALTZED to the STAMPEDE.

The CRAZY GENIE turned all WOMBATS into COLE SLAW while doing YOGA on a SOFA.

It's All Greek
(or Latin, or Arabic . . .) to Me
Samples from Sixth to Eighth Graders

The POLKA player hit the CAMOUFLAGED TAPIR instead of the GONG.

The TOBOGGAN-riding, TOMAHAWK-throwing MOOSE was wearing MOCCASINS while SQUASHING the SKUNK.

GOOBER Gary ate BROCCOLI while doing the WALTZ with a DUMB DACHSHUND who smelled like LIMBURGER TORTILLAS.

20. Nanofiction

As much as we'd like to believe that all of our students love to write, we know the truth: some will find joy in writing all their lives, but many will seldom write again once they are not forced to do so. Depending on personal preference (and often, strengths), writing is either a natural act of human behavior—or an artificial one.

This activity is designed for the reluctant writers in your classes. Why? Because the entire written portion of the assignment can be completed in a matter of minutes, so students are virtually assured of feeling the satisfaction of a completed assignment. For another thing, the sentences in each story do not even have to be sentences. They can be phrases. Or words. And the subject matter? Pure fiction, so there is no pressure to reveal personal information or feelings. Your students won't even realize they are building their literacy skills as they complete their assignments.

We came across the idea for this lesson while strolling through a San Diego bookstore, where we picked up a paperback by Steve Moss titled *The World's Shortest Stories*. Intrigued by the premise, we looked through the book and liked it immediately. Just as quickly, we knew we had a great writing lesson for the following school year.

Here's the plan: Using the guidelines provided by Steve Moss for writing these shortest-of-short stories, each student writes a piece of fiction using *exactly* 55 words. That's all. No more, no less. To accompany their stories, students create a charcoal illustration. Together, they will have a project that even those students who roll their eyes at the word "writing" will have to admit is pretty cool.

Product	A short story of exactly 55 words that includes a setting, one or more characters, conflict, and resolution, and is illustrated with a charcoal sketch representing the story's theme
Materials	• 1 copy of the "Nanofiction Guidelines" handout per student (page 137) • 1 display copy of the "Nanofiction Samples" page (page 138) • 1 display copy of completed nanofiction sample by a middle schooler (page 139) • Charcoal pencils for all students • 2 sheets of transparency film per student • Optional: 1 overhead projector and screen
Time	Two 45-minute class periods—one to explain the lesson and write the first draft of the short story and another class to finalize and share the stories and visuals with classmates; the charcoal sketches can be done in school (art class would be ideal) or at home
Common Core State Standards	Activity meets standards 2, 3, 4, 6, 7, 8, 12, and 14–19 from the chart on page 5.

Activity Steps

1. The Hook

Tell your students that today will be a day unlike any other in their language arts class, because they are going to be allowed—indeed, encouraged!—to break some writing rules that have been enforced all year.

Ask students to raise their hands if their answer is "yes" to the following question: "I really, really, really don't like to write." Select five volunteers from this group of hand-raisers and invite them to stand. Ask each one, individually, what it is about writing that they so dislike. Your answers will probably be along these lines: "It's boring," "I'm not good at it," "I never have anything to write about," or "There are too many rules to remember." Thank your students for their honesty and ask them to retake their seats.

Inform your students that the activity they're going to complete today is called "nanofiction," and ask if the name alone tells them anything about the size and scope of the project.

Display a couple of samples of adult-written nanofiction from the "Nanofiction Samples" handout and conduct a class discussion about how these pieces work. Specifically, ask students if they can identify the conflict and how it is resolved by the story's finish. Ask them to identify the setting. What do they know about the characters? In all cases, ask: "How do you know?" This discussion will help students understand how stories are built, and that even a very short story can have a conflict, setting, and characters, conveyed through well-chosen verbs and details, and that these elements make stories interesting and complete.

"Your task today is to write what is probably the shortest story you have ever written in your life: only and exactly 55 words. Complete sentences are optional." (Pause for cheers!) "Let's get started!"

2. Introduce the Activity

Distribute the "Nanofiction Guidelines" to each student and go over them together. If necessary, clarify the meanings of "conflict," "resolution," "setting," and "character" by referring to these elements in the nanofiction samples you displayed earlier. Share the student sample, "Alligator Troubles," as well as the visual created to accompany this story, and tell your students that once their stories are complete, they will create an illustration to complement it.

One reminder to give to your students: just because they write only and exactly 55 words, the story *still has to follow the guidelines and make sense*. In other words, not just *any* 55 words will do, so they will have to choose carefully and think through their story before they write it. The constraints of this form of writing encourage creativity but are not a license to write nonsense.

You may want to impose a guideline for words that cannot be used ("nice," "pretty," "like") because they are too bland. With only 55 words at their disposal, it would be a shame to waste even a single spot on a lousy word like . . . *like*.

3. Invite Students to Complete Their Own Responses

Have students begin working on their story ideas by brainstorming with classmates. Since the samples shown were diverse in terms of topic, this should give your students the liberty to think of different ways to approach this project.

Because setting and characters are two requisites for this assignment, students may begin by simply listing a variety of settings: the school gym, the planet Mars, a fast-food restaurant, a movie theater, inside a video game, and so on. Then have them do the same thing with character ideas: a kid at Disney World, a soldier at war, a chef at a banquet, a musician during his first solo, a flea on a dog. Thinking about the character and setting together is an effective way to focus students who are lost for a fresh idea.

Once the setting and character(s) are selected, students can take time to think of what the conflict might be, and how it might be resolved. Is it a conflict with another person? An inner conflict when the character's mind is "talking" to itself?

Then it is time to begin writing their essays. Remind students that their first idea might not be their best idea, and that they can always change their choice—we're only talking 55 words—if their initial topic doesn't lend itself to a strong response.

As students begin, walk around the room looking for kids who are still struggling with the four elements of the story. Ask a few guiding questions. ("What types of characters do you like to read about?" "What settings are interesting to you? A haunted house? A NASCAR track?") But don't dwell too much on a student's lack of direction. It can be helpful to let these students read what some of your other students are writing; this often gets their own ideas flowing.

Some students will finish a first draft within 10–15 minutes. When they do, have them read one another's stories to learn from their classmates if the stories make sense and contain the four essential elements mentioned on the guideline sheet. You might also ask that students look for these elements in each other's work:

- Are the verbs and nouns in the story strong and specific? Can you, as a reader, actually get an image in your mind as you read the story?

- Are the characters described well enough that they seem real? Do the characters have any traits or physical characteristics that make them unique?

- Is there a defined conflict as the story progresses, and is it resolved in an unexpected, yet logical, conclusion at the story's end?

A few minutes before the period ends, ask for several volunteers to read their nanofiction to the class. Close the period by telling the students when you expect to see their completed stories and illustrations. We suggest giving no more than two days' time to turn in their finished products, but you may need to allow some time in class for students to work on illustrations if you don't have enough charcoal pencils to send home with students.

On the day the assignments are due, have students gather in small groups to read one another's stories. Collect the stories and illustrations, returning them another day with your evaluative comments. Students may share their work either by posting it in a classroom or corridor, or by transferring their stories and visuals onto overhead transparencies and overlaying them on the projector—a very cool effect.

Extensions

Classroom Extensions

1. Instead of doing this activity whenever you can fit it in, do it in relation to an upcoming holiday—Halloween, Valentine's Day, Thanksgiving. Especially for younger students, or those who struggle with topic selection, this targeted focus can help jump-start their writing.

2. Have students pair up to complete a single piece of nanofiction.

3. For a new twist on the old theme of "what I did on my summer vacation," ask your students to respond in a 55-word essay. For a different twist, ask them what they did not do that they wish they had.

4. Take one of the illustrations completed by a student for this assignment and show it to the entire class. In small groups, have students use this visual as the basis for writing *another* 55-word short story that could apply to this illustration. Ask for volunteers to read aloud their stories.

School Extensions

1. If more than one class completes this activity, invite students to participate in a "NanoSlam." Akin to a poetry slam, students who volunteer will read their memorized nanofiction while the words and visuals are displayed behind them on a large screen. Another adaptation we've used to good effect is setting up a large white sheet backlit by a bright light (for example, a classroom lamp without its shade). As students read their nanofiction, one or two other students pantomime the action from behind the backlit sheet.

2. Ask staff members to write a 55-word description of a memorable teaching event—a lesson that went well (or flopped), a parent conference that left the teacher laughing or crying, or an emotional teacher-student interaction. Post these pieces of "nanofact," one per week, in a staff bulletin or website.

Family Extension

Invite students, together with their parents, to recall a family event that could be written in this 55-word format. Instead of fiction, this "nanofact" story can describe a family vacation, a new pet's arrival at home, or a sibling's departure to a faraway college. These stories can then be displayed adjacent to the students' own stories.

Nanofiction Guidelines

Tiny stories can tell big tales. As you put together your 55-word short story, remember that it needs to include the following elements:

- **A setting**—a physical place where the story happens

- **One or more characters**—a person or people (or animals or aliens, etc.) to act in your story

- **Conflict**—a problem your main character faces

- **Resolution to the conflict**—a logical or surprising conclusion to your character's situation

A few notes:

- Avoid boring words like "nice," "pretty," and "like." Use a thesaurus if you need a strong alternate for a common word.

- Even though your story is fictional, it must still make sense. Think about how your story will end before you start writing it.

- Full sentences and incomplete sentences are allowed.

- In designing your sketch, make sure it fits the theme of your nanofiction.

- Have fun!

Nanofiction Samples

Higher Education

by Ron Bast

"College was a breeze," Jennings said, washing his grimy hands. "With all those budget cuts, they couldn't teach much. They just gave us our grades and sent us on our way."

"How did you learn?"

"We didn't, but so what? Look at me now."

A nurse opened the door.

"Dr. Jennings, you're wanted in surgery."

Chameleon Schlemieleon

by Patric S. Tray

The brainiac. The nerd. Not anymore. A midsemester move to a new school. A chance for a new identity.

Algebra. First day. First period. Sitting in the back with the cool people, hoping to clique, I finish my exam long before anyone else.

Doubting my calculations, the teacher grades it aloud: 100.

I've failed.

The Dance

by Joy Jolissaint

He shuffles to my locker. Skinny Steve with the zits. Yuck! Probably wants to ask me to the dance. My last chance. Oh, well. Better than being a wallflower, like Jenny.

Deep breath. "Hi Steve."

"Hi, Sue."

"You wanted to ask me something?"

Even his zits blushed.

"I wondered . . . do you have Jenny's phone number?"

The Relentless Follower

Two pirates shuffled down the leafy sidewalk, followed by a tall man wearing a suit. The man waited in the shadows whenever the pirates raided a house, demanding candy, but he was always nearby.

"Your dad's starting to give me the creeps," Eric whispered at last.

"Wait," said Pete, "I thought he was *your* dad."

The Family Farm

Five generations of Burkhardts lived and died here. Their tombstones overlook the pond.

Mary and I (the new owners) are renovating the kitchen when three translucent figures appear.

"Welcome, and keep up the good work," they chorus, before floating through the solid stone wall.

Startled, Mary grips my arm. "And if we don't?" she gasps.

Nanofiction
Student Sample

Alligator Troubles

by Brianna, 7th grade

Kindergarten buddies touring the Amazon on a wooden boat. Suddenly . . . alligators! Thrashing, squealing. Both struggle to stay on, trying to avoid falling into dangerous, gator infested waters. Oh! The imagination of kids!

Years pass, calm waters. Still buddies, but the alligators take the shape of different problems.

21. One Life, Six Words: Your Choice

It began with a bet. Ernest Hemingway, whose novels have inspired people's souls, was in discussion with a friend one day about the clean terseness that is a hallmark of his writing. He bet his buddy $10 that he could write a complete story in six words. Not chapters. Not sentences. Six words.

Here's the story he composed:

For sale: Baby shoes. Never worn.

He won the bet.

Some time later—in 2006—several entrepreneurs from the San Francisco area decided to launch *SMITH Magazine* (www.smithmag.net), because they believed that everyone has stories to tell and they wanted to provide a forum for these stories to be readily available. But their journal is unique: Authors are limited to telling their stories in only and exactly six words.

The project sparked a firestorm of interest, so much so that two books of six-word stories were compiled by *SMITH Magazine*'s editors and have become best sellers (*Not Quite What I Was Planning*, 2008, and *Six-Word Memoirs on Love and Heartbreak*, 2009). The stories run the gamut from the humorous ("Silently suffered his facial hair experiments") to the sublime ("Smart, humble, shy. Notice me, please?"), and neither book is entirely appropriate for children. However, the *idea* behind the book is one that knows no age bounds . . . something you will discover when you complete this activity with your students.

Product	A collection of six-word "essays" by each student and a six-colored illustration of one of these essays
Materials	• 1 copy of the "One Life, Six Words: Your Choice" handout for each student (page 143) • 1 display copy of "My Life Revealed in Six Words," completed student responses to "One Life, Six Words: Your Choice" (page 144) • Optional for teacher only: 1 copy of either of the *SMITH* books dedicated to six-word stories, or access to the *SMITH Magazine* website (www.smithmag.net)
Time	Two class periods: one to review the lesson and compose the stories and one to review, illustrate, and display them
Common Core State Standards	Activity meets standards 2, 3, 4, 6, 7, 8, 12, and 14–19 from the chart on page 5.

Activity Steps

1. The Hook

Share with your students these short statements written by sixth graders (write them on the board or otherwise display them):

- Little sisters make for big problems.

- Plays with dog, dog scratches eye.

- They're mean, but that's their job.

Ask the students what these sentences have in common. Most will probably disregard the word count of the sentences and focus instead on the similarity of the topic—perhaps that they all could have something to do with family. Probe further, asking your students to focus more on the structure of the sentences than the content; before long, someone will notice that each sentence is only six words long. At this point, ask, "Well, even in six words, can you get a picture of the writer's opinions or experiences?"

End this introduction by telling your students that their next writing assignment is going to be the shortest on record (even shorter than the 55-word "Nanofiction" assignment on pages 133–139, if they have done that). Your students are likely to be intrigued by the notion of such a "simple" assignment. Little do they know its depth!

2. Introduce the Activity

Ask your students if any of them have ever heard of the author Ernest Hemingway. Surprisingly, many will have not! Mention some of his books (bring in a few, if possible), and, should you be a real Hemingway fan, read an excerpt or two from one of his more accessible works (for example, *The Old Man and the Sea*).

Explain how Hemingway's stories often contain very precise nouns and verbs, with an absence of flowery language and description. Share two quotes on writing from Hemingway:

- "There is nothing to writing. All you do is sit down at a typewriter and bleed."

- "All my life, I've looked at words as though I was seeing them for the first time."

Discuss as a class what he may have meant by these two observations on writing.

Next, share the story of Hemingway's bet regarding the six-word story, and reveal to them the one he composed ("For sale: Baby shoes. Never worn."). Ask for volunteers to talk about the meaning of these sentences, and see if they can identify the source of tension in this story. Tell your students that Hemingway won his $10 bet because he had, indeed, told a complete story in a very short piece of writing.

Distribute copies of the "One Life, Six Words: Your Choice" handout, which contains both the Hemingway story and the assignment guidelines, and review it together. Note that the assignment for students involves nonfiction six-word responses, unlike Hemingway's story.

After you have discussed the handout and answered all questions students have, display or distribute the "My Life Revealed in Six Words" sheet and read several of these together to give your students some ideas as to how this assignment can be done.

3. Invite Students to Complete Their Own Responses

Before students begin completing this activity, impress on them that first drafts are not necessarily the *best* drafts, and that even though this activity looks like it can be completed in ten minutes or so, you want students to consider their words carefully before they write them down. There is no need to finish the 12 statements on the assignment sheet during class time; since the individual assignments are so short, a really strong response might come to them when they aren't even thinking about it—while riding their bike, playing a video game, or stargazing into space! Mention, too, that their friends or family members might enjoy the challenge of six-word stories. If so, offer students extra copies of the handout to share with others. (You could also offer to email it to students who want electronic copies.)

Give students a final deadline several days out, during which they should complete their six-word essays and edit them. Then, have each student select one of their statements and illustrate it using (of course) six different colors of crayons or pencils. The end result will be a six-word wall display chronicling the lives and times of your students and their families.

At some point, perhaps a day or two after you introduce this activity, consider posting in the classroom several published six-word stories and essays you find at the *SMITH Magazine* website, hoping it will prod conversation about what makes a strong response to this assignment.

Extensions

Classroom Extensions

1. If your students appreciate the brevity of this assignment, why not open up or close each class session with a six-word appraisal of the day ahead . . . or the day just passed? Comments such as "Test tomorrow. Anxiety tonight. Relief Friday." Or, if you celebrate birthdays in your class, have the celebrant pick one or more people in class to give a "special six-word greeting" shout-out to the birthday boy or girl.

2. Take a document that is quite long—perhaps the Student Conduct Code for your school—and ask some students to rewrite these

guidelines in six-word statements. Something like: "Running? Shouting? Swearing? Bad ideas, all." The same can be done for your class rules, with an example being, "Bring a sharp mind and pencil." This is a fun way to show the artistry of brevity.

School Extensions

1. For a staff development session or faculty meeting, ask teachers and administrators to submit six-word statements that describe the best aspects of working at this school, or the most rewarding lesson or frustrating moment they have done in their classroom recently. A panel of teacher judges can select the most inspiring, humorous, or honest expressions and provide small prizes to those who wrote them.

2. If your school has daily announcements broadcast throughout the school, make a "Six-Word Statement of the Day" part of them. You can start by selecting statements from your own students and then invite other teachers/classes to create their own. You may have the person who wrote the statement read and explain it, or simply have it posted on the school's website along with the daily announcements.

Family Extension

If parents, siblings, or grandparents took part in this activity, post a chart of their responses outside your classroom during parent conference nights, adding your own six-word thank-you for the advice, guidance, or insight their statements provided.

One Life, Six Words: Your Choice

One of the greatest authors in the English language, Ernest Hemingway, wrote powerful novels with complex characters. But in creating that power and complexity, Hemingway stayed away from flowery language; rather, he wrote simple, direct sentences that grabbed you by the throat and made you sit up and pay attention.

One day, Hemingway made a $10 bet with a friend that he could write a complete, effective story in just six words. His friend took him up on this wager . . . and lost. Here is Hemingway's six-word story:

For sale: Baby shoes. Never worn.

Such can be the power of brevity.

Guidelines

Below are 12 categories. Respond to each one with six words. Don't just write *any* words, though. Take time to consider which are the six best words in our whole language that will get your message across. Keep in mind, unlike Hemingway, you are writing *nonfiction* responses (personal essays).

Once you finish, put your 12 six-word essays away and come back to them in several days to look at them again and revise them. Some helpful revision questions to ask yourself include:

- Do these words get across what I *really* mean to say?

- Is the image I create with my words specific enough that others will understand what I mean?

- How do my word choices create a feeling? Is it the feeling I want to create? How could I change it?

After you've revised your sentences, select one to illustrate on an 8½" x 11" piece of paper using six—exactly six—different colors to express your essay's meaning through drawing. If you would like to ask your parents, grandparents, siblings, or friends to complete their own six-word essays, have them do so on a separate sheet of paper.

Good luck. Have fun. Reveal yourself.

- -

Categories

Your life as a student
_____

Your life as an athlete
_____

Your life as an artist
_____

Your life as a son/daughter
_____

Your life, in summary
_____

Your goals for the future
_____

Your greatest triumph
_____

Your biggest defeat
_____

Your greatest fear
_____

Your biggest wish
_____

Your advice to others
_____

Your advice to yourself
_____

My Life Revealed in Six Words
One Life, Six Words: Your Choice
Answers by Seventh and Eighth Graders

Beautiful pain, many stories, never content.

Started with promise. Ended with dreams.

Two sides. There's more to me.

I'm not found when I hide.

Great families make for greater generations.

Parents will always find things out.

Dark, dramatic, disturbing, poetic: my life.

Basics for survival: eat, sleep, swim.

Spiders all around me. Please help!

I want to be an architect.

Sometimes, I don't wanna go back.

Average, but believing that I'm better.

Worked and chiseled but still imperfect.

A good mixture: happiness and creativity.

Don't let guys ruin your life.

Snakes and geese make me cry.

Love books, love electronics. Conflicted much?

I was lost. I still am.

Dreams tightly held. Even when broken.

I wonder what this button does?

Not always normal but still awesome.

Music reaches people. I make music.

Raised my sister before raising myself.

Sunny with a chance of rain.

Six words will never be enough.

Please let me grow. Shortness sucks.

Change is always a breath away.

The end is never the end.

Reached for the stars. Then further.

So many ideas, so little time.

Does hope always work like this?

22. I Got the English Class Blues

Of all the things that middle school students enjoy, music is sure to be near the top of their lists. Whether they prefer rap or rock, country or classical, the tunes that fill their MP3 players are sure to be numerous.

Teachers can capitalize on this attraction to songs as they prepare language arts lessons. Musical lyrics are a form of poetry that can teach our students about such universal themes as love, loss, hope, and despair. These themes can be as present—and pressing—in a three-minute song as they are in a 250-page novel. This activity is designed to take advantage of students' interest in modern music and show them the common bonds that today's songs share with some music and poetry of another era: the era of the blues.

Product	A collection of original blues poetry accompanied by artwork that symbolizes the theme of the students' written work
Materials	• White construction paper and lots of blue chalk • Access to the website of the Academy of American Poets (www.poets.org) • 1 display copy of the completed student samples of blues poetry (pages 148–149)
Time	Three or four class periods, as well as homework time for revision
Common Core State Standards	Activity meets standards 2, 3, 4, 6, 7, 8, 11, 12, and 14–19 from the chart on page 5.

Activity Steps

1. The Hook

As students enter your classroom, have Beyoncé's version of the Etta James song, "At Last" set up for students to view (search "Beyoncé Etta James" on YouTube). Once the video has ended (about four minutes), ask your students if any of them have heard the song before. Even if they had not heard it before today, ask them the following:

- What do the lyrics suggest this song is about?

- Would you say the song is more about happy or sad times?

- Does the slow pace of the song add to or take away from its message? Why do you think so?

Mention that this song was written more than 40 years ago and that it falls under a certain genre (or type) of music called "the blues." Let your students know that they will be exploring the music and poetry of an earlier time, in hopes of finding some common connection to the music of today.

2. Introduce the Activity

Pair up your students and have them navigate online to the Academy of American Poets website. Have them type in the name "Langston Hughes" in the search window and find the Langston Hughes page, which contains a short biography of the poet as well as links to several poems.

You may wish to first read the biography with your students to get them acquainted with his background. Then direct your students to open the poem "Dreams," a very short poem, and read it to themselves. Ask each pair of students to come up with a word or phrase they think describes the poem's meaning. Expect to hear words like "hope," "optimism," "never give up," "courage," etc. Make a list of the words and phrases students suggest.

Next, have them read the poem "I, Too, Sing America," and again ask for words that describe the poem ("prejudice," "despair," or "hope" are common responses). Follow this with the reading of one final poem, "Life Is Fine," which has a lighter, almost comical tone, and ends with Hughes stating how much he prefers living to its alternative.

Afterward, tell your students that "the blues" is a form of music that evolved at the end of the 19th century and early 20th century in African-American communities. The blues is characterized by certain musical qualities, but also by themes (topics) that are sung about—and these themes are very similar to those common in Langston Hughes's poetry. Blues songs are generally sad laments about hard times and personal difficulties, especially about difficulties within African-American society. Many blues songs feature a single line that is repeated three or four times at various points during the song.

Next, have your students search for the lyrics of several examples of classic blues songs, such as "Honky Tonk Blues" by Jelly Roll Morton, "Cross Road Blues" by Robert Johnson, "Tupelo Blues" by John Lee Hooker, or "Baby Won't You Please Come Home" by Charles Warfield and Clarence Williams (performed by Bessie Smith). You may want to play these songs on YouTube.com as well so the students can listen to them.

End this day's lesson with a homework assignment your students may actually enjoy: finding a modern song that they like that they believe could qualify as "bluesy" in its music and lyrics, and bringing its lyrics to the next class for discussion.

3. Invite Students to Complete Their Own Responses

When students arrive the next day, display a copy of the Langston Hughes poem "The Weary Blues" (also available at www.poets.org), while they view a four-minute musical version of this poem performed by Cab Calloway (search on YouTube.com for "weary blues cab calloway"). Some of the words in "The Weary Blues," such as "syncopated," might not be familiar to your students, but the poem and music should provide enough context that your students will understand the general theme of Hughes's poem.

Once the viewing is complete, ask your students what they believe this poem is about. Also, ask them to notice the following elements in "The Weary Blues": its rhyming pattern, its repetitive stanzas, its rich description ("ebony hands on each ivory key"), and the presence of what songwriters would call a chorus.

Next, ask your students to get into small groups and discuss (for about 15 minutes) the previous night's homework: the song they selected that they believe has some of the same elements as blues music and poetry. Spend a few more minutes having several students mention to the entire class how the song they chose contains themes (for example, love, loss, hope) of many blues songs.

As this discussion winds down, urge students to consider what subject their own blues poem will cover. Suggest two categories from which your students can select: whimsical issues or serious issues. Here are some examples of each:

Whimsical

- The No Allowance This Week Blues
- The Little Sister Blues
- The Dating Two Guys at the Same Time Blues

Serious

- The Dirty Planet Blues
- The Intolerance Blues
- The Divorced Kid's Blues

To give your students a feel for what these finished products might look like, share with them the student created examples provided with this activity. Point out (or ask students to identify) some common elements of these examples: the repetition of certain lines, the presence of a main problem or woe (having no money or losing a best friend), and the rhyming nature of the poem.

It's time now for students to begin work on their own song. You might allow them to work in small groups, if they choose. Sometimes sharing their work as it is being created sends students into a direction they had not anticipated. Once students have completed the first draft of their poems, have them trade with a partner to provide feedback on the content and style of each other's work. A revised draft should be completed for homework.

On the final day of this activity, have your students complete the chalk sketch to accompany their blues creations. (We suggest having students first draw their sketch in very light pencil before putting the final product together in blue chalk.) Remind students that the image they create should represent in a fairly obvious way an element of their poem/song.

Extensions

Classroom Extensions

1. If you have the time and ambition, invite some local songwriters and/or musicians (high school musicians or music majors from a nearby college) to visit the school, meet with your students, and put their poetry to music. As your students sing their blues songs, the invited musicians can play the instrument of their choice to accompany them.

2. Using a program such as Garage Band, have your students put their poems to music and record them. Make a classroom album of original blues tunes and post it on your class website for free download for any family members who want to listen to it.

School Extension

This project lends itself very well to a poetry slam, where the student authors recite or sing their memorized songs to other classes. As an intriguing follow-up, you can do a more "improvisational slam," where teachers or students select topics (for example, "The I missed the bus blues") that are then composed and performed spontaneously.

Family Extension

Email home several of the online references used to complete this activity and ask parents to spend some time reading additional blues poems or listening to some blues music with their teens. You might even suggest they put together a family songbook of favorite blues (or "bluesy") music and poems.

I Got the English Class Blues
Student Samples

I Been Blessed Wit Pain
by Joshua

Lawd, we's a both know I ain't goin' nowhere
   special
Lawd, we's a both know I ain't doin' nothin'
   special
'Cause Lawd, too many times we have to fight
   an' wrestle.

My back is tired and broken
Oh, how my back is tired and broken
But Lawd, we's a both know I ain't puttin' in
   my token.

Lawd, my faith ain't all that strong
Oh, dear Lawd, my faith ain't all that strong
Can you, can anyone, help me carry on?

You been hittin' me wit hailstones all day long
Been hittin me wit hailstones all day long
But I know you's a hittin' me to make me sing
   your song.

Oh, I wish it would rain 'cause I feel like I'm
   a dyin'
I wish it would rain 'cause I feel like I'm a dyin'
Lawd, I wish it would rain so you couldn't tell I
   was a cryin'.

Lawd, this hurts, but don't stop tryin' to break me
Lawd, this is painful, but don't stop tryin' to
   break me
Lawd, I need this pain 'cause I know it's gonna
   get me to praisin' Thee.

Lawd, is you gonna stick wit me 'til the end?
Lawd, is you really gonna stick wit' me 'til
   the end?
Lawd, you think me an' you can be friends?

Dear Lawd, maybe I'm a goin' somewhere special
   after all
Lawd, maybe I'm doin' somethin' special after all
Only 'cause you made me get on my knees
   and crawl.

continued →

I Got the English Class Blues
Student Samples (continued)

No Money Blues
by Ashanti

I got the no money blues, Lord
The bad no money blues.
Got them awful no money blues,
Bad, bad no money blues
Need me some change and greens
To get me some cornbread and shoes

Been lookin' all day for work, Lord
Walkin' up and down this here road
Lookin' hard all day for work, Lord
Up & down, up & down, this here road.
Can't get me no help nowhere
To ease my heavy load.

This pain is mighty hard, Lord.
And I jus' can't find my way.
Guess I'll keep on walkin'
Rest my feet and eat another day.

Best Friend Blues
by Beth

My best friend has replaced me,
With someone I know.
My best friend has replaced me,
With someone I know.
This change is overwhelming,
Like the touch of cold, bitter snow.

I go through every day
Knowing that it won't be the same.
I go through every day
Knowing that it won't be the same.
Because this torn friendship has
Someone else to blame.

This person has dark eyes,
And takes up all her time
This person has dark eyes,
And takes up all her time.
This rocky mountain of friendship
Is becoming very hard to climb.

Someday I will understand
Why she acts this way.
Someday I will understand
Why she acts this way.
I am tryin' to be patient,
And hope our friendship will not stray.

23. A Cento for Your Thoughts?

When it comes to poetry, there are two camps: those who like it and those who don't. Or, at least there are those who *think* they don't like it, for a multitude of reasons. If poetry doesn't rhyme, some adolescents think it is *not* poetic, while others believe that a rhyming poem is tantamount to a greeting card's message: trite and forced. Also, some poems seem to tell a cohesive story, while others seem to ramble without focus. And what about the punctuation? Who decides if a comma comes at the end of each line or not? Indeed, poetry, more than any other written form, seems to have those who embrace it and those who avoid it.

This activity is designed to introduce your students to some of the world's most elegant poetry and to help them create a poem of their own using already published works. In a sense, the poem created by your students will be a form of "plagiarized originality," where the "stolen" words will be a tribute to the original sources. The unique part of your students' creations will be the thoughts that go into weaving a poem composed of the elegant words of other poets who came before them. And, they might just learn a thing or two about the poets whose work they have used as a springboard for their own poetic creations.

We especially like to do this activity near the end of the school year, using it as a reflective way for students to note their own growth throughout the year, or as a boost to launching their hopes for the year or years to come.

Product	An original poem, between 8 and 25 lines, in which every line is the *first* line of an already published poem; this type of poem is called a "cento"
Materials	• 1 copy of the "A Cento for Your Thoughts?" handout for each student (page 153) • 1 display copy of "A Cento for Your Thoughts?" student samples (page 154) • Internet access
Time	Two 45-minute class periods: one to explain the lesson and begin research, and one to complete the research and begin to write poems; some additional time at home might be required for some students
Common Core State Standards	Activity meets standards 2, 3, 4, 6–9, 12, and 14–19 from the chart on page 5.

Activity Steps

1. The Hook

Display the student sample "The Embankment" and read it aloud to your students. After reading the poem once, ask students to close their eyes and listen as you read it again. Immediately thereafter, ask them to jot down on a piece of scrap paper whatever thoughts they have about the poem—were there particular lines they liked? Images that went through their minds as they listened to the poem? Interpretation of what the poem might mean? Be prepared for some students to have a page full of ideas while others will be more perplexed: "I don't know what this poem is about—I didn't 'feel' anything."

Inform the students that they are going to be allowed to do something for today's lesson that they are generally forbidden to do: use the work of others to create their own. "Many people find it difficult to write poetry," you might explain, "so we are going to use some of the world's greatest poets as the source of our own creations."

2. Introduce the Activity

Ask your students to write a number between 1 and 10 on a piece of paper that indicates their "personal poetry index." A 1 stands for "avoid at all costs" and 10 means that they live, breathe, and eat poetry! If they ask (and someone probably will) "What do you mean by 'poetry'? There are so many different kinds," direct them to focus on the types of poetry they know best—rhyming, non-rhyming, humorous, romantic, even song lyrics.

Next, divide the students into groups of four made up of two students with low scores on the "poetry index" and two other students with high scores. Ask each student to explain to the other group members the rationale behind their poetry index rating, being as specific as possible (for example: "I just don't get much poetry; the lines often don't seem to work together" or "I just love how poetry allows you to interpret in ways that are meaningful to you"). After a few minutes, have a class discussion in which you ask students to share responses, positive and negative, to poetry.

Show "The Embankment" once again, explaining that an eighth grader composed this poem using the opening lines of already-published poems. Poems composed in this manner are called "centos." They combine the words of some of the world's greatest poets into a brand-new composition. Show the second version of "The Embankment" that identifies the sources of all the lines.

Tell your students that their assignment is to create a cento that addresses one of two themes:

- How have I changed from the beginning of the school year until now?

- When I think of the upcoming year, what do I hope lies ahead for me?

3. Invite Students to Complete Their Own Responses

Distribute the "A Cento for Your Thoughts?" handout and go over it together. Share with students the other student samples, "A Cricket's Song" and "Gnome-Man's Land." Encourage your students to interpret these two centos, sharing responses with the class.

Students should spend the rest of this first day looking for poems and selecting first lines they might want to use in their own centos. A few good sources for poems include:

- The Poetry Foundation (www.poetryfoundation.org); click on "poetry tool"

- The Academy of American Poets (www.poets.org), which in addition to a large collection of poems also has audio for many poems

- *Poets & Writers* (www.pw.org); click "tools for writers" and then click "literary magazines" to find a list of contemporary journals; students can sort the list so only journals with poetry show up, and then they can click through to journals

- Any poetry anthologies or journals you have

Initially, students can work in pairs as they peruse these sources, copying lines they like into a word processing document as they go. Suggest that they collect dozens of lines, so they will have many from which to choose when they begin composing their poems. Urge them not to be concerned at this time about "which line goes where"; that task will come later.

As your students grow their collections of first lines, they should start thinking about which of the two themes they would like to consider—how they have grown this year or what they hope for the future.

On the second day, give students who need it the time to continue looking for poetic lines that they might want to use in composing their centos. Otherwise, this period should be spent selecting the lines they want to use and arranging them into an original cento. Some students may want to take some extra time, so you may want to assign a due date a day or two in the future so those students can continue working at home.

On the due date, ask your students for suggestions for how best to share their centos with each other . . . and follow their direction. Some ideas might be compiling them into a book, recording them for a podcast, holding a class reading, and so on.

Extensions

Classroom Extensions

1. To add an up-to-date twist to this activity, open up the realm of song lyrics' first lines instead of "literary" poetry. Of course, discretion will need to be used here, since not all lyrics are school appropriate! However, this twist will be a more palatable alternative to those students who have little to no interest in reading or interpreting poetry—unless that poetry was composed by a lyricist whose work they enjoy (and, for sure, song lyrics are a form of poetry!).

2. If interest is strong, students can draw an illustration that complements their cento.

3. Have students choose one of the poets whose work they used in composing their cento and read more of this poet's creations, then write a brief biographical sketch of the person, focusing on how this person's life may have influenced the poems she or he wrote.

4. Sometimes, a poem's final line, or middle lines, are even more stunning than the first. Have students write additional centos using last lines or other lines instead of first lines.

School Extensions

1. Invite several of your colleagues to complete this activity in their classes, followed up by holding a "Centos Slam," in which students retreat to the library and read their poetry in true coffee-shop fashion. If your school website features student compositions, place several centos each week on the site.

2. Lighten up the mood by having students create centos that are all humorous in nature, using such poets as Shel Silverstein, Ogden Nash, and Dr. Seuss. The theme could be "How to have a little fun in your life" or "The wackiest day on record" or some other humorous idea that takes the centos to a fun place.

3. Why not invite your school's staff to complete their own centos and share these on the bulletin board closest to the school's entrance? If desired, the teachers can explain the meaning of their centos, or they can simply be displayed and open for personal interpretation.

Family Extension

Ask family adults to read their student's centos and write a brief note that details their own interpretation of the poem or that asks them questions about the cento's meaning. Attach this note to the cento and give it to your students a week or more after this activity is completed.

A Cento for Your Thoughts?

A cento is a poem that is created by using lines of *published* poems and rearranging them into an *original* poem that is created by you. So . . . it is a form of plagiarized originality!

Your assignment is to compose an original cento of between 8 and 25 lines, choosing one of these themes as you compose your cento:

- A personal look at the person you have grown to become this year

- The person you hope to become in the year or years that follow

Here's how to start:

1. Locate at least 16–50 first lines from published poems (but more is better) that intrigue you or relate in some way to the life you are leading now—or want to lead in the future. Write down these first lines or paste them into a word processing document. These are all *possible* lines for your cento. Also, record the name of the poem and the poet, so you have these for reference later on.

2. Once you have located plenty of lines that seem to go together, look at them all and determine which might be a good one to begin your cento.

3. Then, look at the other lines you've chosen—do any seem to follow the theme of the first line you chose? Continue doing this until you have completed your cento.

4. If you wish, you may use the same line more than once (perhaps to begin and end your cento).

Do not be concerned about whether your poem rhymes—it probably will not. Instead, focus on creating an image or idea that flows from one line to the next in a way that you like. Perhaps your cento will have many references to family, or your love of nature. As long as your cento makes logical sense *to you*—and it helps you reflect on the life you are living today, or the life you hope to lead in the future—you will have completed this assignment as intended.

Here are some resources for finding poems you might use.

- The Poetry Foundation: www.poetryfoundation.org

- The Academy of American Poets: www.poets.org

- *Poets & Writers Magazine:* www.pw.org

A Cento for Your Thoughts?
Student Samples

The Embankment
by Amanda, 8th grade
Over the tops of the houses
Now sleeps the crimson petal, now the white
Mist clogs the sunshine
Over the sea our galleys went
Now sleeps the crimson petal, now the white.

O friend! I know not which way I must look
My hair is grey, but not with years
To toil all day and lie worn-out at night
O Captain! My captain! My fearful trip is done.

The darkness brings no quiet here
Why hast thou nothing in thy face?
Do ye hear the children weeping, o my brothers?
Child of a day, thou knowest not.

A Cricket's Song
Rowena, 7th grade
The heart is a garden
The beginning of the world—
And the end
An angel, robed in spotless white,
The silver charms of his dull art
Glazed with bittersweet raindrops.

The sun has shut his golden eye,
The ancient moon rules star-lit skies.
All white, the cherry blossoms once more
Where youth, the ageless fountain fills.

Starlight and dewdrops waits for thee—
For the moon never beams without bringing
   me dreams.
Purpling shadows drift across the land
A minute to smile, an hour to weep in.
No more to laugh, no more to sing.

Thus weave for us a garment of brightness
A rainbow holds out its shining hand
The cricket's song, in warmth increasing over
Thus made me stronger. I've grown to see
The poetry of Earth is never dead.

Gnome-Man's Land
by Andy, 8th grade
Have you been to the land of happy?
Gnomes dwell there, and goblins, too.
I dwell there and so do you.

What tricks do you know?
Laser vision.
That is your trick? That bit of filthy magic?

I needest not that to survive
My love is all I need
I love rock and roll!

He does just fine.
The boy with the blonde hair
But now and then, he fails.

The Embankment *(Source poems)*
Over the tops of the houses
   *(from "Twilight on Sixth Avenue and Ninth Street"
   by Charles Roberts)*
Now sleeps the crimson petal, now the white
   (from "The Princess" by Alfred Lord Tennyson)
Mist clogs the sunshine
   (from "Consolation" by Matthew Arnold)
Over the sea our galleys went
   (from "Over the Sea Our Galleys Went" by Robert Browning)
Now sleeps the crimson petal, now the white.

O friend! I know not which way I must look
   *(from "Written in London, September, 1802" by William
   Wordsworth)*
My hair is grey, but not with years
   (from "The Prisoner of Chillon" by Lord Byron)
To toil all day and lie worn-out at night
   (from "Living" by John Boyle O'Reilly)
O Captain! My Captain! My fearful trip is done.
   (from "O Captain! My Captain!" by Walt Whitman)

The darkness brings no quiet here
   (from "The railway station" by Archibald Lampman)
Why hast thou nothing in thy face?
   (from "Eros" by Robert Bridges)
Do ye hear the children weeping, O my brothers?
   *(from "The Cry of the Children" by Elizabeth
   Barrett Browning)*
Child of a day, thou knowest not.
   (from "Child of a Day" by Walter Savage Landor)

24. Poems for Shared Voices

Years ago, a nifty and unique little book named *Joyful Noise* by Paul Fleischman brought poetry into the realm of science. In verses meant to be read by two or more voices alternately (and at times simultaneously), Fleischman explained metamorphosis through the eyes of a wannabe butterfly experiencing it, while erosion was witnessed through the antagonists of water and rock, water and rock.

Read orally, these poems resembled more of a conversation than a poetic discourse, and the effect on the listener was powerful. It was almost impossible to listen to these poems and not visualize what was happening to the insects, water, and plants that make up the content of these short, explanatory poems. The hard science of biology became softer when experienced through the rhythm of a carefully crafted verse.

The format of *Joyful Noise* is the inspiration behind this activity. Using the structure of "parallel poetry," wherein two or more students write—and read—a single poem they design together, students bring to life one or more fictional characters in a book that both of them have been reading. Just as each of us has contradictory thoughts and emotions at times, especially under stress or conflict, the fictional characters with the most depth also confront inner conflict. This activity allows these inner voices to speak simultaneously and, in doing so, add some clarity to the confusion of daily life—in fiction or in fact.

Confused? That's okay, as this activity is best explained through example rather than narrative. So, read through the following few pages and then return to this introduction. What is now as clear as mud will become transparent as glass.

Product	Poems coauthored by two or three students that explore a dilemma of a fictional character and are illustrated visually with a poster; each team of coauthors also completes a "Scene Synopsis Sheet" (page 161) that puts the two products into context
Materials	• 1 display copy of the "Poems for Shared Voices: From *Joyful Noise*" handout (pages 158–159) • 1 copy of the "Poems for Shared Voices Guidelines" handout (page 160) per pair of students • 1 display copy of the "Poems for Shared Voices" student sample (pages 162–163) • Posterboard or blank white paper and markers or colored pencils for each pair of students
Time	Three 45-minute class sessions: the first to explain the activity, form groups, and have students select the character(s) and scene they will describe in their poem; the second to write the "Poem for Shared Voices" and draw the poster; the third to rehearse the poems and present them, along with the posters, to the class.
Common Core State Standards	Activity meets standards 2, 3, 4, 6–9, 12, and 14–19 from the chart on page 5.

Activity Steps

1. The Hook

Ask for a student volunteer—a strong reader with a flair for the dramatic would be a good choice—to help you read something that is both simple and complicated—*simple* in its words, *complicated* in the coordination of reading required for the two readers. Project the poem "Grasshoppers" from the "Poems for Shared Voices: From *Joyful Noise*" handout onto a screen or board. It has two columns. You read everything in the left column, while your student volunteer reads everything in the right column (most of the time you'll be alternating turns, but when both columns have words at the same horizontal level, both readers speak the line simultaneously).

If you make mistakes in the first few readings, don't worry. Try it again. You will probably need to read the poem aloud several times before the rhythm flows for you. Once you have mastered the poem, read it with as much dramatic effect as you can muster. Ask for another volunteer to take over your role. Do this several more times, always substituting only one student at a time. After a few readings of "Grasshoppers," do the same thing for the second poem on the handout, "Water Boatmen."

Afterward, ask a few volunteers to discuss how they think this writing and presentation style changes the way a poem affects listeners. Next, ask if they can think of times in their own lives when they wish they could say two things simultaneously, perhaps when they are struggling with an important decision which has more than one solution. End "the hook" by telling your students that it is now going to be their turn to compose a poem in this unique, two-voice style.

2. Introduce the Activity

Tell your students that their task is to compose a poem for two or three voices that helps to explain a character and/or scene in a book they are now reading or have read previously. Show the completed student example, "How Come?", which imagines an internal conversation that two characters from *The Outsiders* have about the differences between themselves, the poor, outcast "Greasers," and the rich, clean-cut "Socs." Ask two students to read this poem and a third to interpret it once the reading is finished. Even if students are not familiar with *The Outsiders*, the poem "How Come?" is vivid enough that they will pick up the gist of its content.

Next, show your students the poster that accompanies "How Come?" and ask if and how it represents the poem's words. If they do not believe it was an effective representation, ask for alternate ideas.

Distribute the "Guidelines" handout and carefully review these points:

- Look for scenes that have specific conflicts or characters that experience powerful emotions or thoughts.

- Make sure you understand the *purpose* of the poem you are writing. What message do you want your audience to understand as they listen to the different voices?

- Decide ahead of time if your characters will try to solve a problem in your poem or simply share their feelings about something that has happened to them in the context of the book's plot.

- If your conversation is actually one character talking to himself or herself, make it clear what specific problem or situation is going through this character's head.

Next, groups are formed—two or three students per group—depending on a fictional book that all students in the group have read.

3. Invite Students to Complete Their Own Responses

Once students have selected their group members and the book they will use for this assignment, direct them to the "Scene Synopsis Sheet" and have them complete this page (except for question 6) and show it to you prior to writing their poem. The more specific the scene or emotion they are trying to describe, the more understandable the poem will be. This will probably be enough for this activity's first day.

To begin the second day, ask the students to begin composing their shared poems, stopping at a couple points as they go to read the lines aloud in their groups and honestly evaluate their work:

- Does the opening clearly establish the characters and situation?

- Do the word choices convey the emotions or struggles or situations the group wants?

- Do the voices alternate in a rhythmic and logical sequence?

- What lines are read simultaneously? What is the effect of this? Could it be improved?

Remind your students that they are not *telling a story* as much as they are *describing how a character (or characters) is feeling about a particular situation*. We have found this advice most helpful for students who are having difficulty with this assignment. Help these students pinpoint a specific *emotion* or *situation*, since limiting their focus is often effective.

When they finish their poems, the students should work on their posters, choosing a scene or idea to illustrate. Refer them back to the "How Come?" assignment to get an idea of how the poem and art can relate to each other and what the art might look like.

On the third class day, have your groups complete question 6 on the "Scene Synopsis Sheet" and perform their poems in class, displaying their posters at the same time. Afterward, the poems and posters can be placed in a prominent place in the school or on a class or school website for others to admire and enjoy.

Extensions

Classroom Extensions

1. If students enjoyed this activity using literature as a base, have them follow the same guidelines using a popular song as the source of their shared-voices poem. The students can play the song in class, followed by their poetic interpretation.

2. Just as fictional characters face issues that make them question their beliefs or cause them to look at life from a variety of viewpoints, your students face such dilemmas as well. Brainstorm a collection of life situations (for example, sharing space with siblings, meeting parental expectations, confronting anxiety in a new sport), and ask students to compose shared-voices poems for these real-life situations.

School Extension

If your school has a peer mentoring program, have your students compile a series of shared poems addressing common issues confronted by kids their age: peer pressure, cheating, dealing with bullying, etc. In classroom settings or at a grade-level assembly, students can talk about these topics, ending each one with a shared poem that addresses the issue under discussion.

Family Extension

After family adults have read the student's shared-voices poems, ask if any of them would be willing to write one *with* their child about a situation commonly addressed between parents or caregivers and kids (for example, completing homework, dealing with loss or disappointment, getting a new pet). Then, if the parents are willing, they may come to class and read these poems with their child. For an added twist, have the child write the parent's voice while the adult composes the child's responses.

Poems for Shared Voices
From *Joyful Noise*

Grasshoppers

Sap's rising	
	Ground's warming
Grasshoppers are	Grasshoppers are
hatching out	hatching out
Autumn-laid eggs	
	splitting
Young stepping	
	into spring
Grasshoppers	Grasshoppers
hopping	hopping
high	
Grassjumpers	Grassjumpers
jumping	jumping
	far
Vaulting from	
leaf to leaf	
stem to stem	leaf to leaf
plant to plant	stem to stem
	Grass-
springers	springers
Grass-	
soarers	soarers
Leapfrogging	Leapfrogging
longjumping	longjumping
grasshoppers.	grasshoppers.

continued →

Poems for Shared Voices

From *Joyful Noise* (continued)

Water Boatmen

"Stroke!"
We're water boatmen
"Stroke!"

             "Stroke!"

"Stroke!"
We're cockswain calling
"Stroke!"

             "Stroke!"
             up early, rowing
             "Stroke!"

             "Stroke!"
             and oarsmen straining
             "Stroke!"

"Stroke!"
and six-man racing shell
rolled into one.

             We're water boatmen
             "Stroke!"

"Stroke!"
worn-out from rowing
"Stroke!"

             "Stroke!"
             Bound for the bottom
             "Stroke!"

"Stroke!"
of this deep millpond
"Stroke!"

             "Stroke!"
             where we arrive

and shout the order
"Rest!"

             "Rest!"

From *Building Strong Writers in Middle School: Classroom-Ready Activities That Inspire Creativity and Support Core Standards* by Deb Delisle and Jim Delisle, copyright © 2011.
Free Spirit Publishing Inc., Minneapolis, MN; 800-735-7323; www.freespirit.com. This page may be reproduced for use within an individual school or district.
For all other uses, contact www.freespirit.com/company/permissions.cfm.

Poems for Shared Voices
Guidelines

A poem for shared voices is just what it sounds like: A poem that is meant to be read by more than one voice. To start this assignment, find a partner (or two). As a group, you will compose one poem together that is meant to be read by two or more people in alternating turns (and sometimes simultaneously).

- Your poem should be at least 30 lines long.

- Make sure that your characters have separate voices, as seen on the examples, although there should also be times when all your poem's voices speak at the same time.

- Set up your poem so one speaker's lines are in a left column and one speaker's lines are in a right column. Lines that are meant to be read simultaneously should be in both columns on the same horizontal line.

- Select a scene or situation from the book you have chosen that contains a powerful or emotional situation. Talk with your group member(s) about which characters would be the best ones to include in the poem's conversation. Once you've selected the characters, evaluate which statements they should say together and which they should say separately.

- Do not make your poem rhyme—this poem is meant to sound like real life.

Complete the "Scene Synopsis Sheet" (leave question 6 blank for now) and show it to your teacher for approval before you begin writing your poem. As you compose your poem, keep these things in mind:

1. Understand the *purpose* of the poem you are writing. What is the emotion or situation you want your readers to understand as they listen to the different "voices" in your poem? Do you want your readers to see that your character is happy, confused, or sad?

2. Decide *ahead of time* if your characters are trying to solve a problem or simply sharing their feelings about something that has happened to them in the context of your book's plot.

3. If your conversation is actually one character talking to himself or herself, make it clear what problem or situation is going through this character's mind.

Once you have completed your poem's first draft, practice reading it aloud with your partner(s) to make sure you like how it sounds. Make any changes you believe would make your poem more understandable or emotional.

After your group has written a poem that you think makes sense and truly represents what your character is feeling, get together with another group and take turns reading your poems to each other and offering feedback to each other. Be ready to revise some of your poem's lines based on the feedback you receive.

Once your group is satisfied with your poem's revision, complete question 6 on the "Scene Synopsis Sheet."

Poems for Shared Voices
Scene Synopsis Sheet

After selecting your book, but prior to writing your poem, complete this sheet and show it to your teacher for approval. Do not answer question 6 now; you'll return to it later.

1. Your team members' names:

_____

_____

_____

2. The name of your book and the character(s) who will be "speakers" in your poem:

Book title:

_____

Character(s):

_____

3. A description of the scene or situation that your poem will describe. Add page numbers, if using a particular scene from the book:

_____

_____

_____

_____

4. What is your poem's title?

_____

5. Why did you choose this title?

_____

_____

_____

Teacher's approval of above plan:

_____

- -

6. What do you like the best about the shared-voices poem you have created?

_____

_____

_____

_____

_____

_____

Poems for Shared Voices
Student Sample

After selecting your book, but prior to writing your poem, complete this sheet and show it to your teacher for approval. Do not answer question 6 now; you'll return to it later.

1. Your team members' names:

   Matt O.

   Ryan S.

   Katie N.

2. The name of your book and the character(s) who will be "speakers" in your poem:

   Book title:

   The Outsiders

   Character(s):

   Ponyboy and Johnny

3. A description of the scene or situation that your poem will describe. Add page numbers, if using a particular scene from the book:

   We will describe a conversation that Ponyboy and Johnny might have had about how different the two groups in the book are (the Greasers and the Socs) and why they might be so different. There are no specific page numbers for this situation. It goes on throughout the book.

4. What is your poem's title?

   How Come?

5. Why did you choose this title?

   During the conversation in our poem, the characters ask repeatedly, "How come?" so it kind of made sense to title it this.

Teacher's approval of above plan:

   Mr. Yanez

- -

6. What do you like the best about the shared-voices poem you have created?

   We like how it flows. Also, we like that every once in a while, lines are repeated. The end is also great as both people say the same thing to each other. Everyone in our group helped put this poem together. Hard to believe, but we actually enjoyed this!

How Come?
Sample Shared Voices Poem

Sitting on the curb
We thought of the Socs and thought
How come?

How come they're so rich

        Us so poor

It's not the money

        It's the feelings
        How come?

How come?
They feel nothing

        We feel violence

They strike
Night and day

        We watch in dismay
        How come?

How come?
They think
They're on top of the world

        And we feel
        As if we are useless

They fight strong

        We fight tough
        How come?

How come?
They fight

        We suffer

They dress fancy

        We dress ragged

They've got more
Than they need

        We have less
        than nothing
        How come?

How come?
We end this talk

        But not for long
        Because we
        Still ask
        How come?

Because we
Still ask
How come?

continued →

Greasers   Socs

Index

Page numbers in *italics* indicate reproducible/display pages.

One-liners by students, 77
Online resources
    alphaDictionary, 129
    cooking measurements, 93
    journaling, 69
    KryssTal Borrowed Words in
        English, 127, *130*
    Online Etymology Dictionary, 127,
        130
    people making a difference, 86
    poetry, 145, 146, 151, *153*
    poster-making tool, 30
    quotations, 46, 60, 95
    song lyrics, 46
    thesaurus, 24
    vocabulary, 105
    word clouds, 99
Open-endedness of assignments, 6
Optical illusions. *See* Visual Enigmas
Optimism, in invitational education, 1
The Other Side of Me
    activity, 28–30, *31–32, 33*
    extensions, 30
    sample responses, *34*
Outsiders, The (Hinton), 56
Oxford English Dictionary, 129

p

Parallel poetry, 155–163
Parks, Rosa, *13*
Passion, poems about, *57*
Pause, writing about, 65–68
People Magazine, 86
Persistence, poems about, *57*
Personal beliefs, writing about. *See* Self-
        examination/self-reflection
Personal expression
    importance of, 6
    See also Self-examination/self-
        reflection
Photographs, taking, 115
Placemats, 97–102
Placing Thanks
    activity, 97–99, *100, 102*
    extensions, 99
    sample response, *101*

Poems, creating
    about kids' issues, 157
    A Cento for Your Thoughts?,
        150–154
    Fibonacci sequences, 120–126
    I Got the English Class Blues,
        145–149
    online resources, 145, 146, 151, *153*
    Poems for Shared Voices, 155–163
    That's Just Like Me!, 24–27
    visual/concrete poems, 103–111
Poems for Shared Voices
    activity, 155–157, *158–159, 160, 161*
    extensions, 157
    sample responses, *162–163*
Poetry Foundation, 151, *153*
Poets & Writers, 151, *153*
Posters, making, 28–34
Pride, writing about, 65–68
Publication and distribution of student
        writing
    brochures, 37
    compiling books, 95
    Help, Hope, Hurray! activity, 86–92
    illustrated children's books, 112–118
    posters, making, 28–34
    story samples, 72, *75, 76*
Purkey, William, 1
Purposes of writing, 4
Puzzles
    Visual Enigmas, 18–23
Puzzles and games
    Fibonacci games, 123
The Pyramid of Personal Qualities
    activity, 54–56, *57*
    extensions, 56
    sample responses, *58–59*

q

Questions/questionnaires
    assessment, 4
    eliciting student responses, 8, 25, 56,
        83, 128
    Getting to Know You—Better
        activity, 8–13
    interview questions, 28, *31–32*
    revision questions, *143*
Quotations, writing about
    Lessons from Hogwarts, 60–64
    My Personal Quote Shield, 46–53
    searching for quotes, 46, 60, 95

r

Real Kids, Real Stories, Real Change
    (Sundem), 86
Recipes, writing, 93–96
Research, activities involving
    Fibonacci sequence, 122–123
    It's All Greek (or Latin, or Arabic . . .)
        to Me, 127–132
    My Personal Quote Shield, 46–53
Resources. *See* Online resources
Respect
    in invitational education, 1
    poems about, *57*
Revisions
    revision questions, *143*
    student activities, 36, 47–48, 105
Road atlas, writing and compiling, 95
"Roger and Jim," *73–74*
Rowling, J.K., 60

s

Schoolwide activities
    banners, 99
    book discussions, 63
    brochures, creating and sharing, 37
    Fib Day, 123
    kids' issues, poems about, 157
    pairing young and older students,
        80, 112–118
    polling students, 56
    quotations and thoughts, sharing,
        48, 66
    recipe-for-life cookbooks, 95
    service projects, 89, *91,* 105
    story or poetry reading (slams), 136,
        147, 152
    That's Just Like Me! extension, 26
    W-a-a-a-a-y Beyond Description
        extension, 103–111
Self-examination/self-reflection
        activities
    The ABCs of Journaling, 78–83
    A Cento for Your Thoughts?,
        150–154
    importance of, 1
    It Gives Me . . ., 65–68
    Lessons from Hogwarts, 60–64
    Me in a Nutshell, 35–43
    My Personal Quote Shield, 46–53
    The Other Side of Me, *34*

About the Authors

Deb Delisle has been an educator for more than 35 years and most recently served as Ohio's State Superintendent of Education. Prior to that, she was a school superintendent, a curriculum director, an elementary principal, a teacher of primary and middle school kids, and a K–12 gifted coordinator. She plays an active role in national and international organizations related to school improvement and served on the Executive Board of the Council of Chief State School Officers. She is coauthor of *Growing Good Kids* and the author of numerous articles on gifted child education and reform-based education.

Jim Delisle has taught gifted children and those who work on their behalf for more than 30 years, including 25 years as a professor of special education at Kent State University. Throughout his career, Jim worked as a part-time teacher of gifted middle school children. The author of more than 250 articles and 16 books, he is a frequent presenter on gifted children's intellectual and emotional growth.

More Great Products from Free Spirit

See It, Be It, Write It
Using Performing Arts to Improve Writing Skills and Test Scores
by Hope Sara Blecher-Sass, Ed.D., and Maryellen Moffitt

Improve students' writing skills and boost their assessment scores while adding performing arts education, creativity, and fun to the writing curriculum. With this vibrant resource, students learn how to use acting and visualization as prewriting activities to help them connect writing prompts to their own lives, resulting in lively, personalized responses. Easy-to-use checklists guide students to include specific elements in their writing and to demonstrate skills that are assessed on standardized tests. For teachers, grades 3–8.

192 pp., S/C, 8½" x 11". Macintosh and Windows compatible CD-ROM.

Your Life in Comics
100 Things for Guys to Write and Draw
by Bill Zimmerman

A do-it-yourself comic book features cartooning exercises and prompts that get boys thinking about important subjects in their lives. Rather than provide the story, the book allows guys to decide what happens by creating words and drawings of their own. Some of the interactive exercises feature completed comic strip panels where boys imagine and write the dialog. Others let guys draw comic strips of their own. Freestyle activities let kids personalize the book and explore who they are. Web extensions point the way to additional fun, interactive resources online. Ages 9–13.

128 pp., S/C, two-color, illust., 6" x 9"

Middle School Confidential™ Series
by Annie Fox, M.Ed.

Middle school can be complicated—added classroom responsibilities, changing family dynamics, fitting into a shifting social scene. Featuring a blend of fiction and practical advice for the middle school years, this series provides the answers kids need in a contemporary, graphic-novel format that will draw in even reluctant readers. Filled with character narratives, quizzes, quotes, tools, and resources, these books are timely and engaging survival guides for the middle school years. Ages 11–14.

96 pp., S/C, color illust., 6" x 8"

Be Confident in Who You Are (BOOK 1)
Real Friends vs. the Other Kind (BOOK 2)
What's Up with My Family? (BOOK 3)

The Complete Guide to Service Learning
Proven, Practical Ways to Engage Students in Civic Responsibility, Academic Curriculum, & Social Action (Revised & Updated Second Edition)
by Cathryn Berger Kaye, M.A.

A treasury of activities, ideas, quotes, reflections, resources, hundreds of annotated "Bookshelf" recommendations, and author interviews, presented within a curricular context and organized by theme. This eloquent, exhilarating guide can help teachers and youth workers engage young hearts and minds in reaching out and giving back. The included CD-ROM has all of the reproducible forms from the book plus a new section on how to create a culture of service, 11 new author interviews, and 45 new "Bookshelf" entries. For teachers, grades K–12.

288 pp., S/C, illust., 8½" x 11". Macintosh and Windows compatible CD-ROM.